Enabling Reflective Learning in Lifelong Career Guidance

I0887716

Edited by
Ruggiera Sarcina, Simona Marchi, Furio Bednarz, Massimo Tomassini, Galina Markova and Francesco Consoli

Routledge
Taylor & Francis Group
LONDON AND NEW YORK

First published 2013
by Routledge

2 Park Square, Milton Park, Abingdon, Oxfordshire OX14 4RN
711 Third Avenue, New York, NY 10017

Routledge is an imprint of the Taylor & Francis Group, an informa business

First issued in paperback 2018

Copyright © 2013 Taylor & Francis

This book is a reproduction of *Reflective Practice: International and Multidisciplinary Perspectives*, volume 12, issue 02. The Publisher requests to those authors who may be citing this book to state, also, the bibliographical details of the special issue on which the book was based.

All rights reserved. No part of this book may be reprinted or reproduced or utilised in any form or by any electronic, mechanical, or other means, now known or hereafter invented, including photocopying and recording, or in any information storage or retrieval system, without permission in writing from the publishers.

Notice:
Product or corporate names may be trademarks or registered trademarks, and are used only for identification and explanation without intent to infringe.

British Library Cataloguing in Publication Data
A catalogue record for this book is available from the British Library

ISBN13: 978-0-415-83753-8 (hbk)
ISBN13: 978-1-138-38332-6 (pbk)

Typeset in Times New Roman
by Taylor & Francis Books

Publisher's Note
The publisher would like to make readers aware that the chapters in this book may be referred to as articles as they are identical to the articles published in the special issue. The publisher accepts responsibility for any inconsistencies that may have arisen in the course of preparing this volume for print.

Contents

Citation Information

The chapters in this book were originally published in the *Reflective Practice: International and Multidisciplinary Perspectives*, volume 12, issue 2 (April 2011). When citing this material, please use the original page numbering for each article, as follows:

Chapter 1
The Reflect-OR project: background to the special issue
Ruggiera Sarcina, Francesco Consoli, Massimo Tomassini and Elisa Cavicchiolo
Reflective Practice: International and Multidisciplinary Perspectives, volume 12, issue 2 (April 2011) pp. 151-158

Chapter 2
Temporariness in appreciative reflection: managing participatory and appreciative, action and reflection projects through temporary organisations
Simona Marchi and Ruggiera Sarcina
Reflective Practice: International and Multidisciplinary Perspectives, volume 12, issue 2 (April 2011) pp. 159-177

Chapter 3
Co-constructing an appreciative and collective eye: appreciative reflection in action in lifelong career guidance
Simona Marchi
Reflective Practice: International and Multidisciplinary Perspectives, volume 12, issue 2 (April 2011) pp. 179-194

Chapter 4
Opening PAAR spaces in Bulgaria: reflective accounts
Galina Markova, Haralan Alexandrov, Nadejda Angelova and Silviya Yordanova
Reflective Practice: International and Multidisciplinary Perspectives, volume 12, issue 2 (April 2011) pp. 195-208

Chapter 5
Login and logout: practices of resistance and presence in virtual environments as a kind of reflective learning activity
Simona Marchi and Emma Ciceri
Reflective Practice: International and Multidisciplinary Perspectives, volume 12, issue 2 (April 2011) pp. 209-223

Chapter 6
Reflection on building appreciative memory
Elisa Cavicchiolo and Simona Marchi
Reflective Practice: International and Multidisciplinary Perspectives, volume 12, issue 2 (April 2011) pp. 225-241

Chapter 7
Facilitating capabilities through reflection: from welfare to appreciative well-being
Francesco Consoli
Reflective Practice: International and Multidisciplinary Perspectives, volume 12, issue 2 (April 2011) pp. 243-250

Chapter 8
Empowering people through reframing: experiences of guidance practitioners in a public network of career centres
Massimo Tomassini, Antonella Barile, Eleonora Fiumara and Paola Scarpello
Reflective Practice: International and Multidisciplinary Perspectives, volume 12, issue 2 (April 2011) pp. 251-263

Chapter 9
Reflective practice, appreciative regard and organizational wellbeing: an experience in Swiss employment services
Furio Bednarz, Elisa Cavicchiolo, Simona Marchi and Massimo Tomassini
Reflective Practice: International and Multidisciplinary Perspectives, volume 12, issue 2 (April 2011) pp. 265-279

Notes on Contributors

Harlan Alexandrov works as Researcher and Consultant in the Bulgarian Institute of Human Relations and as Assistant Professor in the New Bulgarian University, Bulgaria. He holds a Masters in Bulgarian philology, a PhD in social anthropology and a second PhD in organizational studies from the Centre for Psycho-Social Studies, UWE Bristol, UK. His academic interests are in the fields of education, social policy and organizational theory. He is involved in various community development and research projects, applying participatory approaches such as action research, reflective practice and cooperative inquiry.

Nadejda Angelova is a member of JobTiger's team – a leading recruitment and career counseling agency in Bulgaria. She is been a Global Career Development Facilitator [GCDF], certified career counselor and trainer by NBCC International (US) since 1995, and now designs and conducts trainings in the field of HR and managers' development. She is also an extreme sports practitioner and loves to challenge people to do their best.

Antonella Barile comes from a social studies background and engaged in career guidance activities for about fifteen years. At present she is a Career Guidance Officer at the Simonetta Tosi Work Guidance Centre of the Municipality of Rome, Italy. In her role, Antonella integrates consulting and counselling competencies, according to the holistic-gestaltic approach of the Atmos Institute for Art Therapies from which she received a counselling diploma in 1996 after a three-year course.

Furio Bednarz is President and Responsible for R&D by ECAP Foundation Switzerland and President of the Conference of CVT Organisation of Italian speaking Switzerland. His research focuses on labour market and workplace evolution, migrations, competence development and innovative training and experiential learning methods.

Elisa Cavicchiolo is a Junior Consultant at Reflective Learning Italy. She has a degree in social and demographic statistics with a thesis on workplace safety (focusing on sociological and organizational dynamics). She has experience in tutoring, facilitating laboratory testing, and the transfer of action research and PAAR (participatory and appreciative action and reflection) methodologies. She also has experience in operational support activities, desk analysis, data analysis and interviews in research projects. Her interests are orientated to professional practices, organizational dynamics, communication, professional and learning change, continuing to cultivate even the statistical field.

Emma Ciceri is Marketing Specialist at Postel SpA, Poste Italiane Group (www.postel.it). She graduated in philosophy from the Statale University of Milan, Italy, and has an internet business- oriented certificate achieved at Pirelli campus. As a member of the innovation team in Postel, Emma has addressed the study of new services and products linked to Web 2.0 resources development and has analysed social networks and marketing dynamics. In particular she developed, at a theoretical and practical level, new online fundraising methods by means of reports and relationships between the non-profit world and contributors' universe. She has collaborated to integrated communication projects development and proposal (direct marketing online and offline) for public and private companies. Her passion for innovative tools, together with a careful and receptive gaze towards new media, represent the hallmark of her work. Previous publications include Emma's co-authored work, *Participatory and appreciative adult learning and reflection in virtual environments* (2011).

Francesco Consoli has been Associate Professor of Sociology of Organization, Sociology of Professions and Sociology of Innovation at La Sapienza, University of Rome, Italy. He has a long experience in reflexive practices and methodologies in teaching and training. In this field he published several articles and books on education and reflective practices. He participated in two Leonardo da Vinci Projects: 'Reflect' (2004-2006) and 'Reflect-OR' (2009-2010).

Eleonora Fiumara is a Career Guidance Officer at the Municipality of Rome, Italy. A psychology graduate, she specialises in systemic-relational psychotherapy. She has over 20 years' experience dealing with training, guidance and counselling issues in private and public services for employment.

Simona Marchi is the General Director of SMILE Italy (System, Methodology, Innovation, in Education) and President of Reflective Learning Italy, 2008-2012. She was a Temporary Researcher at La Sapienza, University of Rome, Italy from 2001 to 2009 and has authored papers on research methods, reflective learning, participative change and innovation in organizations, learning by using web resources.

Galina Markova, PhD. is Director of Know How Centre for Alternative Care for Children at the New Bulgarian University. She graduated from the doctoral program of Smith College School for Social Work, USA and her research is in the field of child welfare and de-institutionalization of services for children, program evaluation in post-totalitarian context, international social work. She is also an Educator and Clinician in private practice

Ruggiera Sarcina is a Senior Consultant, Facilitator, Researcher and Vice President of Reflective Learning Italy. Her main fields of expertise concern project management, action learning and facilitation techniques especially in the framework of European projects, small- and medium-sized enterprises (in particular, aggregation path for innovation and internationalisation projects) and local development.

Paola Scarpello is currently a career guidance officer at the Municipality of Rome, Italy.

Massimo Tomassini is a Social Scientist and Mindfulness Trainer. Massimo is Contract Professor at the University of Roma 3, Italy (teaching organisational learning) and Associate Fellow at the Institute for Employment Research, University of Warwick, UK. With the latter he is at present partner in a transnational research aimed at interpreting individual work and learning paths in different contexts. As a private consultant, he carries out both counseling activities and mindfulness training workshops for individuals and groups.

Silviya Yordanova is a career consultant with JobTiger Ltd.

The Reflect-OR project: background to the special issue

Ruggiera Sarcina[a], Francesco Consoli[a,b], Massimo Tomassini[c] and Elisa Cavicchiolo[a,b]

[a]*Reflective Learning Italy, Rome, Italy;* [b]*Department of Economics, 'Sapienza' University of Rome, Rome, Italy;* [c]*University of Roma Tre, Rome, Italy*

The article introduces the path, the actors and the contexts of the Reflect-OR Project. Reflect-OR is a Leonardo da Vinci Transfer of Innovation (TOI) project developed in the framework of the Lifelong Learning Programme (LLP) and promoted by the European Commission. Reflect-OR aimed at sustaining the empowerment processes of career guidance practitioners by supporting a major awareness and use of their individual, organizational and networking resources. The Reflect-OR project is the transfer of a previous Leonardo da Vinci project called Reflect which experimented with reflective methodologies with teachers and trainers. The path was characterized by an active process of transfer of innovation, constantly constructed and negotiated with the various life-long career guidance (LLCG) practitioners and agencies and based on a creative methodological approach called Participatory and Appreciative Action and Reflection (PAAR). Another important aspect was constituted by the peculiarities of the different contexts involved in the transfer process (Italy, Switzerland and Bulgaria) which allowed a deep reflection on LLCG systems and created a common background for reframing and empowerment.

The Reflect-OR project is a Leonardo da Vinci Transfer of Innovation (TOI) project, co-financed by the European Commission as a lifelong learning programme (LLP). The LLP programme is an umbrella programme integrating various educational and training initiatives. It is divided in four sectoral sub-programmes and four 'transversal' programmes. One of its sectoral programmes is Leonardo da Vinci, which is devoted to vocational education and training. It addresses both the learning and teaching needs in the sector, and is therefore aimed at all parties involved, namely trainees in vocational education, teachers and trainers, institutions and educational bodies, enterprises, associations, social partners and bodies relating to either lifelong learning or the labour market. The aim of the TOI is to improve the quality and attractiveness of the European vocational education and training (VET) system by adapting and integrating innovative content or results from previous Leonardo da Vinci projects or from other innovative projects into public and/or private vocational training systems and companies at the national, local, regional or sectoral level. Such an aim is highly coherent with the objectives of important European Programmes (CEU, 2004; EC, 2008; CEDEFOP, 2008; OCDE, 2004).

Reflect-OR aimed to sustain the *empowerment* processes of lifelong career guidance (LLCG) practitioners by supporting a major awareness and valorisation of their individual, organisational and networking resources. In particular, the idea was to improve and make more effective the CG job through reflective practice methodologies that can lead the operators to a structured reflection with tangible improvement results, regarding both purposes and modalities of their own action and personal involvement. Reflective practices take into account professional experience as a key factor in the lifelong learning processes for practitioners. Reflective practices refuse a separation between theory and practice in favour of the development of a 'professional practice theory'.

Reflect-OR is the transfer of a previous Leonardo da Vinci project called Reflect, which experimented reflective methodologies with facilitators (teachers and trainers) in Belgium, Bulgaria, Italy, the United Kingdom and Romania, and it has left behind it a set of tools and experiences, also transferrable in the guidance context (Figure 1).

We view the transfer of innovation as an active not a passive process. As something that has to be constantly (re)constructed and (re)negotiated with the various lifelong career guidance (LLCG) practitioners and agencies. If this fails to happen, 'transfer' can become another form of oppression. When Horton and Freire (1990) used the phrase 'we make the road by walking', they touched upon a key reflective process. That is the art of learning as we go along. This is an important feature of Reflect-OR. It also reminds us that the process of transfer is not imitation, but the creative application of what we know, brought into creative dialogue with the historical moment. The creative application of participatory and appreciative action and reflection (PAAR), which is a strength-based reflective methodology (Ghaye et al., 2008) enables us to learn as we go along (Figure 2).

PAAR is an emergent form of reflective learning that involves a change in mindset away from deficit-based discourses, towards more strengths-based conversations (Ghaye et al., 2008). To ignite this change, we needed to use the power of the *appreciative question* to build better futures from aspects of the positive present (Thatchenkery & Metzker, 2006). Questions of this kind are aligned with authentic participation, an appreciation of individual and collective gifts and talents, an understanding of the complementary way in which creative and critical thinking interact and the need for moral courage and ethical behaviours. The successful transfer of innovation, through PAAR, required those involved to develop their appreciative 'gaze', their ability to re-frame current realities, create an ethical space where collective wisdom can be developed and which enables individuals and agencies to demonstrate achievement and move forward with conviction.

The title of the field book published at the end of the Reflect project was *Reflective Journeys*. This project has also been a journey: a learning process aiming to support the successful transfer of innovation to enhance lifelong career guidance practice, given by individuals and agencies in Italy and Bulgaria. Enhancement is defined as a 'sustainable improvement in guidance practices'.

During its two-year life, the Reflect-OR project involved carrying out fieldwork activities and workshops in Italy, Bulgaria and the UK that included aspects of the PAAR methodologies, LLCG practitioners and policy makers.

The project has been realised by a multi-disciplinary transnational partnership, composed of the following organisations:

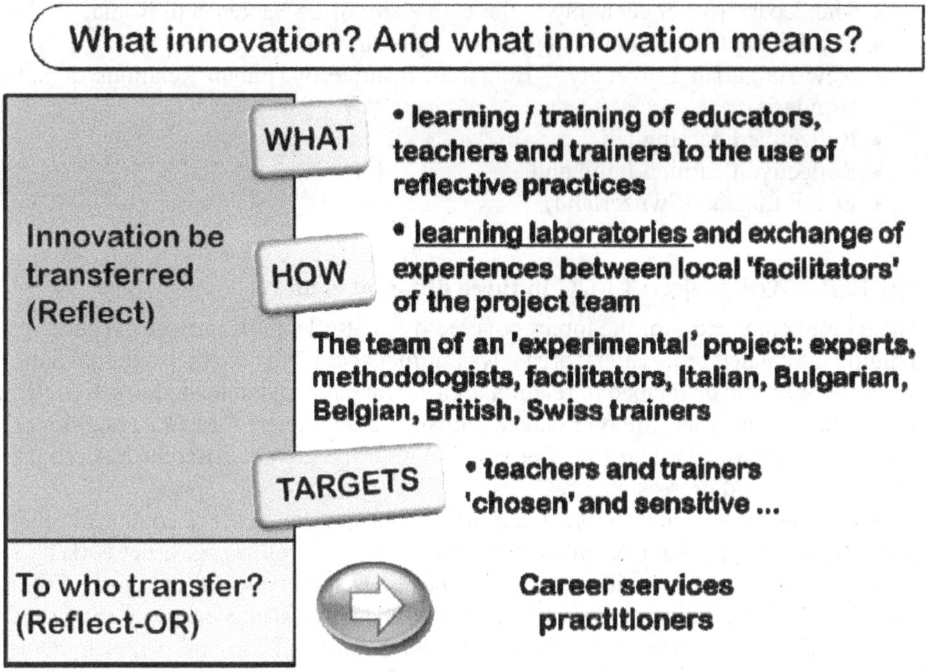

Figure 1. Reflect: the earlier innovation transferred.

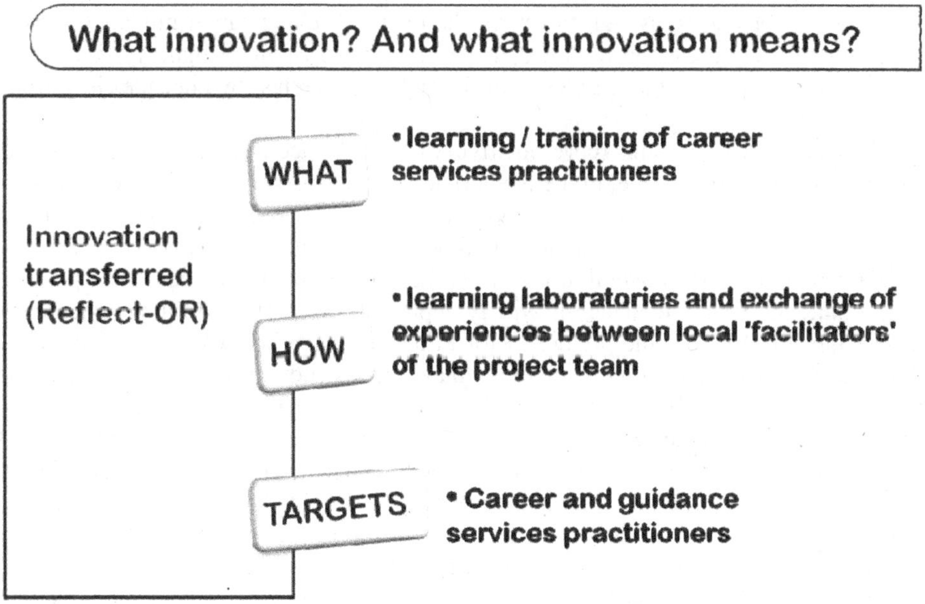

Figure 2. Reflect-OR: the innovation transferred.

- IRSEA (Research Institute on Learning Economy and Society, Italy);
- The Italian Centre of Salesian Works for Women (CIOFS-Lazio) (Italy);
- The Municipality of Rome with its *Centri per l'Orientamento al Lavoro;*
- *Centri per l'Orientamento al Lavoro* (COLs);

- The department of economy at the University of La Sapienza di Roma;
- The Foundation Institute Guglielmo Tagliacarne (Italy);
- New Bulgarian University – Bulgarian Institute of Human Relations of Sofia (Bulgaria);
- Reflective Learning UK;
- Reflective Learning Italy; and
- ECAP Lugano (Switzerland).

The Reflect-OR project: LLCG in three different contexts

The overall complexity of the topics covered by the Reflect-OR project – regarded as a highly articulated professional area – was further accrued by the transnational nature of Reflect-OR and developed in relation to different national contexts. In each of them a generic title such as 'lifelong career guidance practitioner' ('LLCG practitioner') can be translated according to different meanings and covers different institutional, organisational and professional realities.

The project has been developed in a limited but significant set of contexts in Italy, Bulgaria and Switzerland. Such contexts have been the following: a network of 17 small centres for work guidance (*Centri per l'Orientamento al Lavoro* – COLs) established by the Municipality of Rome; a VET and guidance centre also based in Rome (the CIOFS-Lazio); a newly established network of job and career guidance institutions initiated within the New Bulgarian University in Sofia; and a VET and guidance centre (ECAP) in Lugano (Italian-speaking Switzerland) funded by the government of the Ticino canton. Despite the quantitative limits of such contexts, they can be considered as significant for the overall lifelong career guidance system in Europe, as they can be assumed as representative of three main stages of the evolutionary trajectory that LLCG went through over the last two decades in Europe (see references).

The Swiss case seems representative of an advanced area, including LLCG systems in Northern-Europe, in the Netherlands, in Germany and in other contexts, in which adult guidance is a fully developed function. The allocation of guidance tasks to private services that adopt modern methods for guidance counselling appears as a fundamental pillar of an overall transformation process that has already taken place in these contexts. Such a tendency is widely deployed, for instance, in the Netherlands, where the shift towards the private sector in the guidance field can be considered as fully realised, following ad hoc governmental policies and measures. In Germany, on the other hand, the public function of LLCG is still dominant but a recent reform has transferred LLCG, together with other labour policy domains, from a centralistic (at the level of Länder) dimension to a smaller dimension, closer to local exigencies (under the responsibility of municipalities), and has provided incentives for the development of LLCG private services as well.

Swiss public structures play an important role in adult guidance services in VET and in other labour domains but within a delegation system. The cantons tend to retain the rule-generation and planning responsibilities while the practical policy implementation is attributed to bodies belonging to the so-called social-private sector. ECAP, one of the Reflect-OR partners, is an example of such social-private bodies acting on the basis of specific contractual agreements with the cantonal government. Therefore ECAP workers formally operate within a private framework but their activities are highly dependent on the cantonal regulations concerning the ways in which the LLCG 'users' (unemployed people, or at risk of unemployment) must be 'taken in charge' for guidance and, in some cases, for training.

The Italian partners (COLs and CIOFS) can be assumed as representative of a second area of LLCG development conditions in Europe, mostly concerning the Mediterranean countries, where guidance services are in a phase of accelerated transformation. These services have gained increasing levels of social recognition (under the push of difficult labour markets situations) and attracted specific reform policies. However, the transformation processes are incomplete and several delays and malfunctionings are still in place.

In Italy, in particular, an important reform of the public placement services was launched in the mid-1990s also entailing significant improvements of activities and resources for adult guidance. As a consequence of such a reform, the vast majority of guidance activities are now under the responsibility of provincial employment services, but the latter have not yet developed the full range of strategies and technical instruments needed for effectively perform such activities. In a limited number of territories other structures than the provincial services are appointed for performing LLCG. The Municipality of Rome, for instance, has created a network of centres for labour guidance (*Centri di Orientamento al Lavoro* – COLs) whose tasks are mainly related to providing both useful information for jobseekers and job and career counselling for those willing to deepen their own talents and opportunities. COLs' operational conditions are complex, even contradictory, as they must be open to all potential users (including potentially critical target-groups such as dropouts, long-term unemployed, etc.) but at the same time they are not supported by adequate infrastructures and, on the contrary, are ruled by rigid bureaucratic criteria.

The other Italian case, CIOFS-Lazio (a private centre for guidance and vocational education and training belonging to a larger non-profit organization, CIOFS, and held by Salesian nuns) represents a more stable reality, in many ways close to the private-social model of LLCG service provision. CIOFS usually acts as contractor to the Lazio region and of other public bodies for adult guidance activities linked to VET interventions (paralleling its typical activity area constituted by VET courses for disadvantaged young people). CIOFS guidance practitioners tend to keep their professional characteristics, even through specialised tools (such as competence balance), but are largely influenced by their operational context, which is mainly oriented towards education and training goals.

The Bulgarian case represents another kind of condition, typical of Eastern European countries. In these countries LLCG is largely in a nascent state and as a whole it is still not ready for facing the large-scale transformations of work and social life that followed the fall of previous socio-economic systems. In the past regimes, work was granted through top-down processes, structurally far from the idea that in various ways underpins LLCG of a possible matching between individual competencies and attitudes and work opportunities. No specific structure was therefore in place for adult guidance. In the present phase, on the contrary, guidance systems are very much needed in order to respond to the emerging labour markets' exigencies. And of course they have to be built up starting from difficult conditions at both the structural and the cultural level. The institutional structure in this field has to face the persistence of old cultural attitudes towards work and individuals' participation in work processes. Some innovations are at present carried on in order to try to implement new guidance structures and techniques. The Bulgarian Institute for Human Relations (Department of the Sofia New Bulgarian University), a partner in Reflect-OR, was the co-ordinating body

	COLs (Roma. I)	CIOFS-Lazio (Roma. I)	ECAP (Lugano. Sw)	BIHR-NBU (Sofia.Bg)
Type of organization	Network of public career guidance centers of the Municipality of Rome	Local center belonging to a non-profit organization in the field of career guidance and vocational education and training (held by a Catholic order)	Local center belonging to a Swiss Foundation in the field of both career guidance and vocational education and training (originally created by an Italian trade-union), contracting with the Ministry of Labor in the Ticino Canton	Network of start-up or experimental guidance activities, financed by the Bulgarian Ministry of Labor and co-ordinated by the Bulgarian Institute for Human Relations, within NBU (New Bulgarian University)
Date of creation	1997	1958	1970	---
LLCG reference	Middle development of LLCG	Middle development of LLCG	High development of LLCG	Low development of LLCG
Goals	Information for jobseekers and career counseling	Information and career counseling, mostly related to VET interventions	Career counseling (and support to training in some cases)	Implementation of experimental settings for career counseling
Major activities	First reception, orientative counselling, support for enterprise creation, assistance for stage and job, projects	First reception, orientative counselling, support for enterprise creation, professional courses for young people	Support in job access, professional training, job placing, active in LL training	Orientative counseling
Type of access for clients	Free access for all citizens	Free access for all citizens	Addressed by the public employment service	Free access for all citizens

Figure 3. Synthetic scheme about the different contexts.

of different experiences in this field and was involved in attempts to import advanced guidance tools and methods within such a conflicting context.

It is evident that in the three so-far briefly sketched realities, LLCG has to face different structural conditions. LLCG practitioners, as a consequence, have to play context-specific roles and to inhabit structurally specific spaces in terms of social recognition, self-identity and professional growth (Figure 3).

Despite these differences, the project succeeded in creating a common background for both the reframing of activities and relations in LLCG centres and, supported by the PAAR approach, the identification of 'a better future' for each of them. At the same time, the project created significant spaces for partners' mutual understanding and for new transnational relationships aimed at common development purposes.

References

Council of the European Union. (2004). Draft resolution on strengthening systems, policies and practices in the field of guidance throughout life in Europe, 9286/04/May.

European Centre for the Development of Vocational Training (CEDEFOP) (2008). *From policy to practice. A systematic change in lifelong guidance in Europe.* Thessaloniki: Cedefop Publications.

European Commission. (2008). Employment in Europe. Brussels: DG Employment, Social Affairs and Equal Opportunities.

Ghaye, T., Melander-Wikman, A., Kisare, M., Chambers, P., Bergmark, U., Kostenius, C. & Lillyman, S., (2008), Participatory and appreciative action and reflection (PAAR) – Democratizing reflective practices. *Reflective Practice, 9*(4), 361–397.

Horton, M., & Freire, P. (1990). *We make the road by walking: conversations on education and social change.* Philadelphia: Temple University Press.

Organisation for Economic Co-operation and Development (OECD). (2004). Career guidance and public policy. Bridging the gap. Geneva: OECD Publications.

Sultana, R., & Watts, A. (2006). Career guidance in public employment services across Europe. *International Journal for Educational and Vocational Guidance 6*, 29–46.

Thatchenkery, T., & Metzker, C. (2006). Appreciative intelligence: Seeing the mighty oak in the acorn. San Francisco: Berrett-Koehler.

Watts, A., & Sultana, R. (2004), Career guidance policies in 37 countries: Contrasts and common themes. *International Journal for Educational and Vocational Guidance 4*, 105–122.

Temporariness in appreciative reflection: managing participatory and appreciative, action and reflection projects through temporary organisations

Simona Marchi[a,b] and Ruggiera Sarcina[b]

[a]*Department of Economics, 'Sapienza' University of Rome, Rome, Italy;* [b]*Reflective Learning Italy, Rome, Italy*

The time dimension has become increasingly important in organisational management studies. Various concepts have been developed: *temporary work, temporary systems, projectification* and *temporary organisations.* Many aspects have already been studied; for example, relationship structures, the characteristics of projects that temporary organisations (TOs) intend to implement and develop, legal forms, the different sectors in which TOs have been disseminated, and the degree to which they have been formalised. However, one aspect that has still not been studied in depth is the specificity of their temporariness and the specificities of the organisational, social and learning systems that this encourages.

In this paper, we consider a temporary organisation as an organisation composed of teams belonging to two or more non-temporary organisations (NTOs) collaborating to achieve a certain objective and giving themselves a precise structure and roles and a set timescale established *ex ante*. The paper seeks to answer the following questions:

- What were the characteristics of the Reflect-OR project, as 'read' through a TO lens?
- What type of relationships take shape in TOs between the two qualities of persistence and temporariness, and what effects do these have on individual and organisational learning?
- In what way does the *ex ante* limited timescale affect participants' empowerment?
- How does the specificity of the TO affect social processes and the results achievable?
- What characteristics should a participatory and appreciative, action and reflection (PAAR) TO have, i.e., a TO that helps generate systems of activity within which learning and reflection can be appreciative, democratic, participatory and ethical?
- What type of project management do TOs require?

Introduction

The time dimension has become increasingly important in organisational management studies. Various concepts have been developed: temporary work, temporary systems, projectification and temporary organisations (Perrow, 1991; Midler, 1995; Kenis, Janowicz-Panjaitan, & Cambré, 2009). And many aspects have already been studied; for example, relationship structures, the characteristics of projects that temporary organisations intend to implement and develop, legal forms, the different sectors in which they have been disseminated, and the degree to which they have been formalised. However, one aspect that has still not been studied to any great extent is the specificity of their temporariness. Before examining why this aspect is important for the purposes of studying individuals' and organisations' participation, reflection and learning processes, we should first select a definition of temporary organisation. For this, we refer to *Temporary organisations* (Kenis, Janowicz-Panjaitan, & Cambré, 2009). The authors state:

> We defined temporary organisations as two or more non-temporary organisations collaborating to accomplish a joint task with the duration of the collaboration explicitly *ex ante* fixed, either by a specific date or by the attainment of a predefined task or condition. (Kenis et al., 2009, p. xiv)

> An organisation might be defined as an autonomous work system governed and managed through a system of rules, regulations and procedures. However, interorganisational temporary organisations are not organisations in the classical sense since they are composed of independent and sovereign organisations collaborating mainly to contribute to a common task. (Kenis et al., 2009, p. 2)

Very often, in the context of experiences developed at the local, national and international levels, project participants find themselves working in interorganisational TOs that have the above-mentioned characteristics (suffice to mention the projects funded as part of the lifelong learning and transfer of innovation (TOI) strand). And just as often, as professionals engaged in planning, managing and implementing actions and initiatives, we take for granted the organisational forms through which these activities are developed. European projects, for example, require a partnership structure to be established that takes on specific roles and responsibilities in order to achieve certain goals. These structures are in turn configured in such a way as to maximise their chances of obtaining the funding applied for. They must therefore pay close attention when completing the project paperwork and take into proper account the project assessment criteria set out in the tender notices. So partnerships, team structure, goals, roles, responsibilities, products, paperwork and assessment criteria all must be taken into consideration in configuring the specificities of interorganisational temporary organisations (ITOs). The situation is taken to extremes in the case of public funding but is not really so very different in private bids. However, we very often operate as though this new ITO generated on a functional basis with respect to objectives to be achieved (which ones, exactly?) was not already, right now, an active entity, in action, the embodiment of a specific organisational culture. What relationship is there between this performing narrative established *ex ante* for ITOs and the organisational and work cultures of the non-temporary organisations from which they are composed?

Learning processes are closely connected with the characteristics of the social-technical and normative contexts in which professional and day-to-day practices are implemented. They develop from and through different activity systems (Engeström, Miettinen, & Punamäki, 1999). These systems are made up of subjects acting on the basis of explicit and implicit rules in order to achieve given objectives, through the use of artefacts and knowledge and within a specific system of division of labour, definition of roles and power mechanisms. What happens to learning mechanisms in the relationship between temporary and non-temporary organisations? What is the best way to manage/facilitate ITOs whose tasks are learning and the improvement of the professional practices of participating actors whose 'day jobs' are in a variety of non-temporary organisations?

The observations made thus far prompt us also to consider the relationship between ITOs and non-ITOs with respect to the type of interactions and relationships that can be activated. We also know how important the type of relationship and interaction is with respect to participation/exclusion and trust-building mechanisms, and with respect to the ethical dimension. This leads us to ponder the relationship between the roles and practices performed within non-ITOs and those performed in temporary interorganisational teams created within ITOs.

What characteristics do we find in groups working within an ITO? Are the teams focused on achieving an objective? Are they collectives of professional practices aiming to share practices and professional experience? Are they communities of practices whose goal is learning? Within the relationship between the temporary and non-temporary organisations concerned, what types of relationships are established between participants? Are they colleagues, participants in a learning pathway or partners in learning? What outcome is produced through this meeting of what may be very different organisational and work cultures?

In this paper, therefore, and in view of the above, we consider it important to introduce the concept of temporariness in the context of what has been defined as the PAAR approach – participatory and appreciative action and reflection (Ghaye, 2008). We seek to highlight how the participation, appreciativity, action, reflection and space dimensions are configured and how they can be managed ethically within the ITO experience.

Some initial questions

Why is the concept of ITOs useful in a reflection on the introduction and management of PAAR learning and of individual and organisational development processes? To understand how learning and individual development within an ITO combine with and/or differ from what happens in organisations that will continue to exist even after the tasks in question have been completed (organisations conceived as institutions that must continue to exist). 'Every action must be undertaken with respect to eternity' (Weick, 1974, p. 499). How are organisational actions and those of their members affected when the intention of existing for eternity no longer holds? Which kind of relationship exists between the two forces of persistence and temporariness in organisational learning and individual development?

Individual and organisational learning and development experiences are increasingly characterised as temporary and interorganisational initiatives. This is linked to project culture, funding mechanisms, the 'public tender' and assessment system approach, partnership characteristics, the methods of constructing and managing internal leadership structures and group functions (project team, task force, participants).

Is it possible to consider a typological representation of the specificities of temporary organisations? With respect to which variables?

This is an aspect that has not yet been studied in any depth in organisational theory and which has focused primarily on non-temporary organisations. Working-by-projects within a temporary organisation produces different effects on expectations, learning (outcome and methods), practices, behaviours and attitudes with respect to what would happen in a non-temporary organisation. The time element does not so much explain learning and behaviour, but is an important variable with respect to which interorganisational temporary organisations are structured through a specific system of rules, resources, division of labour and instruments to achieve certain objectives. What is the role of temporariness with respect to the functioning and outcomes of temporary organisations?

To study in depth if and how it is possible to develop, through a temporary organisation, an appreciative and participatory learning and reflection approach to improve the quality of participants' working conditions, interaction and working practices, is important to understand the role of time and temporariness in organisational learning. What role do temporary organisations play in generating systems of activity within which learning and reflection are appreciative, democratic, participatory and ethical? How does the limited duration, established *ex ante*, impact on participants' empowerment?

In the project management literature time is viewed as a scarce resource that needs to be managed strategically to achieve the set objectives. However, the literature does not examine how an awareness of the limited duration of the project affects expectations (and how these change over time), or how it helps generate and modify interactions and relations between interorganisational actors. The hypothesis is that an *ex ante* awareness of the limited duration of the organisation affects the perceptions, expectations and conduct of the participants involved, and as a result the functioning of and results achieved by the entire TO. What impact do limited duration and temporariness have on the social processes and results obtained by TOs? What type of project management do TOs require?

Temporary organisations, initial definitions and reflections

Interest in temporary organisations (TOs) is not new, indeed it first emerged in the second half of the 1960s. One of the best-known works moving in this direction is *Theatre as a temporary system* (Goodman & Goodman, 1972), which, as the name suggests, refers to theatre productions. The main sector in which the concepts of first, temporary systems, and second, temporary organisations, began to spread is industry (engineering, construction, architecture, theatre and film-making). After the 1980s the TO concept also began to appear in the public sector and in the profit and non-profit third sector.

The increased attention that the subject attracts is related to the development of project-based organisational forms and the development of participatory forms of leadership to co-ordinate work teams with respect to achieving specific goals. The factors emerging from this type of literature, from the outset, concern the need to devise organisational forms such as TOs with a greater capacity to adapt and change than non-temporary organisations (NTOs). These can be analysed by considering the nature of the goals, project duration, the characteristics of the working group or team, and the variety of organisational and leadership styles.

Some features of TOs

> …a set of diversely skilled people working together on a complex task over a limited period of time. (Goodman & Goodman, 1976, p. 494)

> …limited in duration and membership, in which people come together, interact, create something, and then disband. (Moreley & Silver, 1977, p. 59)

> …structures of limited duration that operate within and between permanent organisations. (Keith, 1978, p. 195)

> …bringing together a group of people who are unfamiliar with one another's skills, but must work interdependently on complex tasks. (Bechky, 2006, p. 3)

> …separate legal and financial entities set up for a specific project and dissolved upon its completion. (Whitley, 2006, p. 78)

The different definitions have four common elements: limited duration; one or more tasks to achieve, which are the reason for which the TO is set up; one or more teams interacting and working on the task(s); the production of change through action; and the completion of tasks(s). To these can be added variations on the theme such as the complexity of the tasks; the level of uncertainty as to whether the objective will be met; the interdependence of team members; limited resources (time, instruments, budget); the degree of red tape within the TO; leadership style; methods and styles of communication; levels of complexity of intra- or interorganisational TOs; level of isolation and/or interdependence of the TO with respect to the organisational contexts to which the team members belong; and the selection of team members.

If we consider these elements, then we can say that the Reflect-OR European project was most definitely developed by setting up an interorganisational temporary organisation (ITO). This process came up against many challenges on a case-by-case basis:

- the overall duration was limited (two years) and established *ex ante*;
- the tasks and outcomes were numerous and characterised by different levels of complexity, for each of which a timescale for elaboration, production and completion was established within the total duration of the project;
- the team structure was organised in a diversified and complex manner given the presence of different bodies: project management team, project team, task force, methodological team, other participants;
- the members of this team came from different types of organisation: public-sector institutions; private-sector organisations; profit and non-profit associations. All had different organisational models: network, by project, by function; and operated in different national and international regions (Italy, UK, Switzerland Bulgaria); and
- the national and organisational cultures of origin were very diverse.

Given the nature of the main task (i.e., to develop innovation through learning processes), it follows that improving the quality of each person's work and working environment through learning and reflective practice and the assessment of the project's impact, performance and final outcomes was a far-from-simple process that required dedicated methods of action and specific instruments to be developed.

How did we manage and facilitate all of this?

Towards ITO typologies

To answer the questions posed in this paper and move forward in the reflection, we need to examine certain typological aspects of TOs. By considering types, we can achieve two objectives. First, we can focus on the themes for which it would be useful to retrace the steps of the Reflect-OR project to 'place' it and compare it with the findings of the literature on TOs. And second, we can draw up a model of reflection to help understand, as far as possible *ex ante*, what type of TO we want to generate and/or are helping to generate, for what objectives and through which processes.

By further developing this reasoning, Janowicz-Panjaitan, Bakker, and Kenis (2009) identified a number of key themes which make it possible to cluster the written contributions found in the TO literature. These are:

- *TOs and contingent effects*, which enable us to explore TOs by considering the relationship between their constituent elements and the nature of the objectives;
- *TOs and performance*, which enable us to explore TOs with respect to the variables that have an impact on their effectiveness and on the success factors for the project;
- *Learning in TOs and knowledge flows*, which enable us to explore TOs with respect to learning methods and knowledge transfer within the TOs and between them and their contexts of reference;
- *TOs and human resource aspects*, which enable us to explore TOs with respect to selection, leadership and human resource management methods and achieve clarity in defining roles with respect to objectives;
- *TOs and structure and co-ordination*, which enable us to explore TOs with respect to their structure and the way they are managed and co-ordinated;
- *TOs and decision making*, which enable us to explore TOs with respect to the decision-making methods adopted;
- *TOs and dynamics*, which enable us to explore TOs with respect to the way they evolve over time; and
- *TOs and project-based organisations*, which enable us to explore TOs with respect to their specificity, i.e., that they are project-based organisations.

A specific ITO case: trans-national co-funded European projects

In this scenario, international projects financed or co-financed from public resources are a special case. The European Union, for example, has made the promotion of transnational projects not just one of the key channels for the implementation of its sectoral policies (for example, research and development, lifelong learning) but also a key instrument in supporting the creation of communities that straddle national borders and thus facilitate the construction of truly European innovation processes. Exemplary, in this regard, is the promotion of a European Research Area (ERA), which pools together researchers and networks involved in R&D projects developed on a transnational basis (European Commission [EC], 2007).

European-funded projects have certain unique features that affect their 'non-temporary organisation' dimension:

- the project's life cycle; and
- the project's multi-stakeholder framework.

Project proposals are presented following a public call for proposals using pre-defined templates: at least three partners from three different European countries can apply; a leading partner organisation signs the contract with the European Union or the national agencies representing the EC at national level; cooperation among partners – the consortium – is formalised in a partners' agreement.

The entire project life-cycle is governed by pre-identified common steps that involve, briefly:

- Step 0: Pre-project. The preparation and planning of the project proposal and the establishment of the consortium.
- Step 1: Implementation and on-going monitoring and evaluation. This step involves the implementation, management and on-going evaluation of the project work-plan.
- Step 2: Reporting. Interim and final reporting to the EC and/or national agencies sets out and clarifies achieved, on-going and final results and deliverables and their consistency with planned aims, objectives, defined resources and timing.
- Step 3: Exploitation and mainstreaming. Since these are projects co-funded from public resources, exploitation and mainstreaming are amongst the most significant criteria in assessing the projects' effectiveness and results.

In many cases, the projects must also be seen to comply with certain guiding principles of the European Union: for example, gender equality, the involvement of disadvantaged regions, etc. European projects have another specific characteristic concerning the actors and stakeholders involved. They can typically be considered as multi-stakeholder initiatives bringing together sectoral experts, methodologists, direct beneficiaries (i.e., those target groups the project was developed for), public, semi-public or private organisations having some direct or indirect interest in exploiting or mainstreaming the project's results (e.g., local development agencies, SME associations, social partners, etc.). The EC is part of the stakeholder network as well as the direct 'client' of the project consortium.

Implementing European projects brings out three potential ITO core groupings, each of which strongly characterised by the prevalence of certain dimensions of inter-organisational temporality.

The core partners' grouping

This is constructed at the direct initiative of one or more experts or specialists who bring together the interest and commitment of colleagues with whom, in general, a pathway for cooperation has already been agreed. In terms of duration, the grouping can be disbanded once the bid is submitted. If the project proposal does not receive a favourable assessment, and therefore fails to attract co-funding, the grouping breaks up but not before carrying out a rigorous self-assessment of whether there is any possible room for improvement for subsequent collaborative projects, etc.

Generally, one of the core partners acts as project manager. The core partners' grouping usually enjoys strong organisational and decision-making autonomy with respect to its parent company (NTO). It performs a guiding role in step 1, in general it is directly responsible for step 2 and it co-ordinates step 3.

The project partnership (consortium)

Roles and tasks are assigned to the consortium on the basis of members' complementary areas of expertise. Its composition is in general defined by the core partners' grouping. It may have both a very strong interorganisational dimension and a very strong inter-cultural dimension: partners come from very different regional contexts and highly diverse organisational cultures. While it may contribute to steps 0 and 2, the consortium's key role is mainly expressed in steps 1 and 3.

Enlarged partnership with local stakeholders' network

Nearly all projects have a strongly contextualised local dimension both for implementation or testing and for exploitation and mainstreaming. Both during the implementation stage, when project activity on the ground is envisaged (e.g., training sessions, pilot group testing, etc.) and at the exploitation stage, local partnerships with the stakeholders' network are one of the key characteristics of European projects, and connote and qualify their effectiveness and impact.

Although closely related and part of the same project pathway, the three organisational core groupings (core partners, consortium, enlarged partnership with local stakeholders' network) may each have different characteristics that are still, however, peculiar to the ITO dimension.

ITOs as a participatory and appreciative action, reflection and learning entity

Reflect-OR, a European Transfer of Innovation (TOI) project, was configured as an interorganisational temporary organisation (ITO) with a complex and not easily measurable objective to achieve (TOs and Contingent Effects; TOs & Performance): namely, to improve the quality of lifelong career guidance practitioners' work and working life by learning new methods of reflection and action starting from their own working practices (see Table 1).

As a project group we therefore found ourselves at a starting point where we had identified an objective (broken down into numerous micro-objectives and stages) that initially, on average, was well defined (at least we thought that was the case). The objective was difficult to measure empirically (even though we had thought of a set of 'project success' indicators) since the level of change/innovation that the project was intended to achieve could not be brought into clear focus *ex ante*. This was especially true from the task sustainability perspective, considering the specificity of the organisations involved. The objective drew on a previous experience in another European project (Reflect – Leonardo da Vinci), which in part involved the same partners and in part did not, in part the same methodological approach and in part not; in part the same objective and in part not. To achieve the objective, we planned to use a clearly defined methodological approach.

As this was a TOI project, in these steps we had already produced a double implicit equation: past experience as innovation; transfer of innovation as a learning process. Moreover, as it was a project-based ITO, we initially produced a project that, in view of its binding nature with respect to the funding body in terms of timescale and output, assumed a top-down normative role from the outset (Learning TOs & Knowledge Flows; TOs & Decision Making). Thus, even before entering into its operational stage, our project-based ITO was already producing effects on

Table 1. Interorganisational temporary organisation (ITO).

Organisational dimension	ITO peculiarities
Core partners: micro dimension	This is the ITO dimension that is most stable over time and whose information, decision-making and co-ordination flows, as well as its work flows, are most stable over time. The fact that the team members have an essentially similar background and experience makes it easier to define and agree on common objectives. Learning and organisational learning processes are intensive, thanks not least to the strongly trust-based links and relationships. Members of the group act as a true performance community, i.e. a community that does not just work together but works together to achieve something in common, a truly learning organisation (Franz & Sarcina 2009). This is the core team that generally takes on the role of gatekeeper in the external acquisition of ideas, methods and technicalities; it is in general the core team that performs the co-ordination and overall leadership function.
Partners' consortium: meso dimension	In the consortium, competences and roles are defined during the bid preparation stage, which is in general planned using standard project-planning tools. Potentially uncertain elements that could influence effectiveness and performance levels may emerge in individual participants' NTO parent companies. Indeed, over the 2/3-year average duration of a European contract, the project team members' parent organisations may redefine their organisational structures or development strategies. So they may, for example, redefine or question their degree of commitment to or expectations *vis-à-vis* the project. In such cases, the ITO is not fully isolated from its environment and stresses and this could affect its overall performance. Communication processes are in general discontinuous and tend to intensify as the project milestones draw near. Complementary skills and expertise among the consortium members, personal engagement, a safe, transparent and trustworthy working and co-operation framework are some of the key factors that encourage and support knowledge flows..A dedicated Quality Plan is required as part of the overall project workplan and this is in general defined and carried out following standard prescriptions and rules.
Enlarged partnership with local stakeholders' network: macro dimension	This is the ITO dimension that is potentially most indeterminate (roles and 'engagement' of local stakeholders) and most fragile with respect to external stresses. The perception of dispersion among local teams can be very marked, and prevent or slow down overall knowledge flows (between consortium and enlarged partnerships in the various regions involved in the project). Moreover, it is the enlarged partnership dimension that can produce the greatest stimuli for the on-going refinement of the project.

expectations, goals, learning processes, roles, rules, inclusion/exclusion methods, communication processes and groups. Many aspects of ITOs can be considered in an informed and intentional manner in order to configure a temporary organisation, monitor it throughout its life-cycle and change it when necessary. This means also considering reflection as an organising process (Reynolds & Vince, 2004) for the purpose of ITO development. How?

Some of the elements classified above are consistent with an approached based on the development of participatory and appreciative action and reflection (PAAR). The PAAR approach responds to an attempt to construct a positive frame for everyday individual and professional action. It is a way to recontextualise and reformulate relationships by developing a point of view: a different, positive way of looking at others and at work.

The PAAR label, which is new, was coined by Tony Ghaye (2008) and is described in the text: *An introduction to participatory and appreciative action research: Some principles and processes*, which was subsequently taken up and developed in the article entitled *Participatory and appreciative action and reflection (PAAR) – democratizing reflective practices* (Ghaye et al., 2008). This new approach points to the convergence of theoretical and practical traditions that refer to action methodologies, most notably action research (AR) and participatory action research (PAR).

The roots of PAAR can be found in appreciative inquiry (AI) (Cooperrider & Srivastra, 1987; Cooperrider & Whitney, 2005) and especially in the quest for that which is positive – that which functions well in organisations and individual work. The aim of AI is to discover what breathes life into an organised system (person, organisation, society) at those times when it is most vital, most effective, most constructive and capable/competent in economic, ecological and human terms. AI is based on the practice of formulating questions that reinforce the ability of people, groups and organisations to understand, anticipate and increase their positive potential. This involves mobilising people in the research (positive questions, positive inquiries) and in reflection. It is an approach that emphasises listening and relationships as principal factors in bringing out people's different perspectives and viewpoints: it enables participants to construct a way of thinking in relation to others. The PAAR approach retains critical reflection as the method of analysis used to construct a sense of the reality and characteristics of a given context. At the same time, however, it does not consider critical reflection as the only mode of reflection on which to base action choices. This should be viewed in the context of an appreciative approach that tends to focus on successes and strong points, and to accentuate an emancipatory, positive and creative way of looking at problems (Ghaye, 2008). This in turn implies a need to act in such a way as to channel into the action any new possibilities opened up by appreciating and valuing, in the present, that which proves to be positive.

Reflective learning, as we consider it here, is based on an appreciative reflection, i.e., a type of reflective thinking that aims to identify, value and transform/expand the scope of meaning that is most appropriate for a given group of participants, and to emphasise the conditions in which this occurs. It is an intentional process. The social context in which the process unfolds acquires a vital importance; the experience of individual participants and of the group is recognised and appreciated; participants are no longer just users but active participants whose objective is learning, transformation and improvement at the individual, group and organisational levels. In the course of the Reflect-OR project we were able, as project team and task force, to test the critical points, apparent contradictions and paradoxes of a PAAR approach developed through an ITO. This is especially true with respect to the dynamic evolution of a project, the variability in the organisational contexts to which the groups of

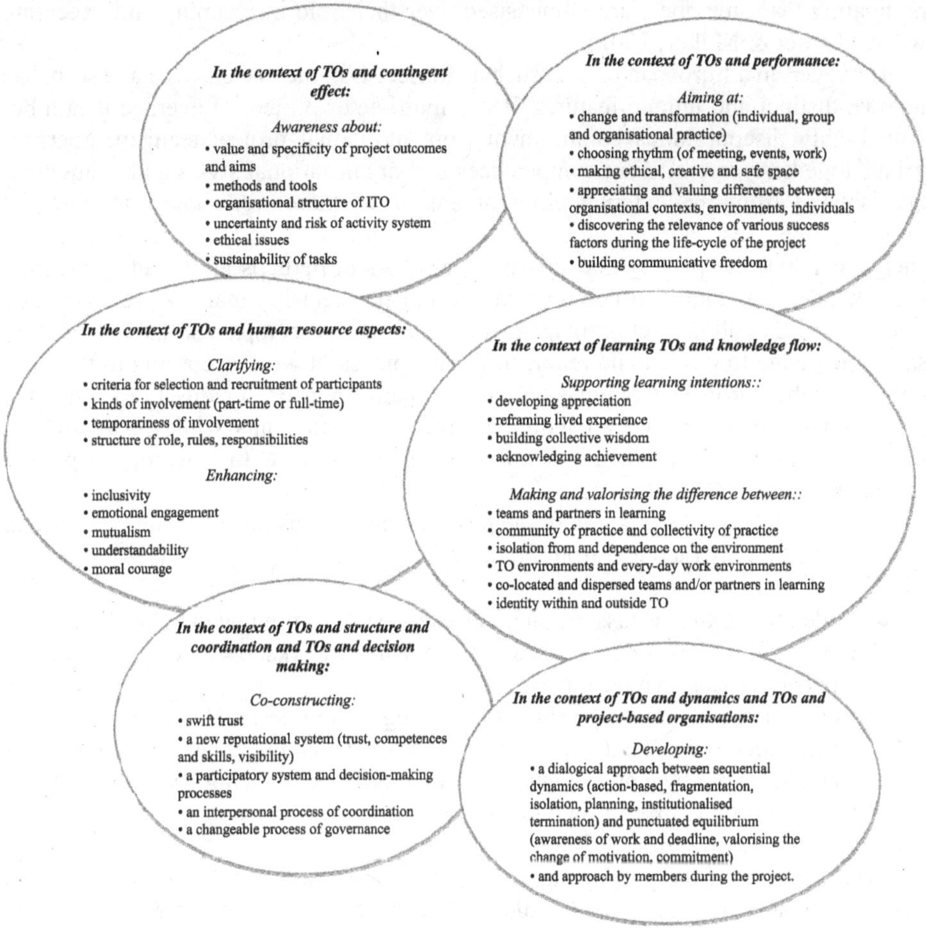

Figure 1. Is a PAAR project-management process for ITOs possible?

participants belong and the constant trade-off between the potential for knowledge integration within a TO and the sharing of knowledge with the parent organisation. We had occasion to appreciate the strong points of this approach, which, along with the problems that emerged through a reflection triggered by the typological model presented in the previous section, have enabled us to take a step forward in defining an ITO as a PAAR entity.

On the basis of our observations thus far it remains to be understood whether and how it is possible to design a PAAR project-management process for ITOs (see Figure 1).

A PAAR project management approach

If we consider a project as a temporary organisation, the project manager is chief executive of the temporary organisation, and thus their roles in objective-setting and motivating team members are emphasised over their role in planning and executing work. (Turner & Muller, 2002).

However, in a European project such as Reflect-OR, the ITO, as we have seen, has its own distinct and unique features. It is a multi-actor project of average length but with highly discontinuous commitment from individual project team members. It brings together very different competences and organisational styles and is anything but isolated from the external environment. It is, therefore, subject to potential unpredictable stress, not just interorganisational but often deeply intercultural too. In such a context, the project manager must also – and perhaps above all – integrate competences and facilitate communication and the decision-making process. They must ensure that all project participants (and their parent companies) have the necessary knowledge to govern and report their own pieces of work according to the rules defined by the European Commission (i.e., the main 'sponsor' organisation). And they must assist – including on an individual basis – participants while preventing or resolving any conflicts that might arise during the project. In a word, the project manager acts as ITO facilitator.

In their role as project facilitator the project manager has different sub-roles which she or he could play (adapted from Franz & Sarcina, 2009):

- moderator with the task of shaping successful communication in the project partnership in general as well as in its meetings, workshops, etc.;
- expert in process management;
- trainer of project management and reporting techniques; and
- coach, since she or he pursues a specific way of shaping enhanced communication and avoiding conflict while, at the same time, being expert at settling conflicts if they arise in such processes.

What happens if the project-based ITO is governed and managed according to a PAAR approach, that is, a methodological approach that emphasises listening and relating to others as the principal factors helping to bring out the different perspectives and viewpoints? How does the project manager's facilitation function change?

To understand this, we trace out, for each ITO dimension, the key characteristics of a PAAR project management process, as emerged after the Reflect-OR two-year project.

The following 'extracts' of reflections, narrations and visual interpretations that participants at the kick-off meeting for the Reflect-OR project shared with their colleagues a few weeks after the meeting are examples of the features peculiar to PAAR project management. Participants were asked to reflect on their 'most significant moment' during the three days of co-ordination meetings.

Example 1: The power of positive questions

In his or her function as facilitator-moderator of meetings and workshops for the project group, the project manager needs to be able at all times to ask the right questions at the right time. Consistency, timeliness and the 'rhythm' of the questions are among the factors critical to the success of the meetings. In adopting a PAAR style, the shift is towards positive questions, i.e., questions that start from appreciation and valorisation – for example, of participants' talents and expertise, of the results achieved, of the opportunities offered by the project, and so on (see Table 2).

Table 2. Interorganisational temporary organisation (ITO) dimensions.

ITO dimensions	Key emerging characteristics of the PAAR project-management process
TO and contingent effects	The project-management process radically changes perspective: from problem-solving process to appreciative process that draws and builds on the team's strong points and unexpected outcomes (e.g. in communication flows and instruments). 'Leaving yourself space to be surprised' by innovations and unexpected outcomes becomes one of the most significant features of this ITO dimension. The PAAR process values and builds upon the competences and talents present in the partnership, regardless of the formal role assigned to individual project team members. Roles performed in the course of the project can therefore evolve and change, in ways that may diverge considerably from the planned course of action.
TO and performance	Strong emotional links and a trust-based cooperation process reinforce the identity of the ITO, not least with respect to the external environment, and, in so doing, the ability to resist external stresses. The group of core partners tends to extend to include, in some cases directly, stakeholders and project beneficiaries. This changes and enriches the decision-making process by: encouraging a slower pace in the process itself and in accomplishing its various steps. It also encourages the inclusion of alternative operational outlooks and options, while still respecting the project's aim and objectives. In evaluating the degree of 'success' of the project, the decision-making and project outcome co-construction process, the quality of communication within the partnership, and the degree of commitment and 'ownership' that develops among participants all acquire an entirely new significance.
TO and knowledge flows and HR aspects	The most powerful driver for the learning process becomes the sharing of 'appreciative' stories and experiences. Here, the project manager-facilitator performs a key role to ensure that the necessary time and space requirements are met, for example by organising regular workshops by project group members. It is, after all, through workshops – therefore regular opportunities to meet – that not only is the process of constructing a collective body of wisdom speeded up but role interchangeability is fostered, especially the role of gatekeepers of new ideas and innovations. At the same time, the 'part-time' dimension of project participants' commitment and the strong geographical dispersion which is one of the projects' main characteristics may threaten to weaken the appreciative learning and knowledge flows or make them extremely fragile. Hence the need for instruments and sharing arrangements that seek to feed or facilitate the PAAR process 'at a distance' (for example, the sharing of written self-assessment narratives).
TO and structure and co-ordination and decision making	The need to support and facilitate the construction of an authentically PAAR process means that a greater number of co-ordination workshops and meetings are required within the project framework. The different modes and styles of communication characterising each project team member must also be respected. The agenda of periodic co-ordination meetings – true milestones in the project-management process – is built up naturally by defining the objectives to be achieved while also leaving a degree of flexibility in the overall schedule. The project manager must also be ready to 'take a step back' by delegating the facilitator role to other participants. The project-management and co-ordination process is structured as a peer-to-peer stewardship.

Table 2. (*Continued*).

ITO dimensions	Key emerging characteristics of the PAAR project-management process
TOs and dynamics and TOs as project-based organisations	In a PAAR project-management process, the early stages of the project are of vital importance in building bonds of trust and activating an ITO that emphasises active listening, participation and appreciativeness. From this perspective, the project kick-off meeting is undoubtedly the first milestone in the PAAR project-management process. The following examples serve to illustrate what makes project management based on PAAR principles so unique: • co-facilitation by the project manager and an expert in methodology; • a flexible agenda that from the outset is open to participation and indeed to members of the project group taking a leading role; • the inclusion in the key stages of the decision-making process not just of consortium partners but also of local stakeholders (enlarged partnership); and • the use of facilitation tools that invite participants to 'exercise' their appreciative reflection process after the meeting and share the results with the group.

Learning to ask the right questions...

The most strong feeling I have of our March meeting was to be engaged in a cooperative and increasingly conscious effort to move from a conversation based on problems and deficits to an appreciative style.

In spite of our 'good (reflexive) intentions', and our previous experience it has not been so easy because the 'attractiveness' of the deficit and negative style of thinking and acting is very strong. But it is still stronger the attractiveness of the problem based conversation.

It is like as it were the easiest path of conversation: something we have the habit to agree is the right thing to do and others expect we are telling about too.

Each time that happened during the meeting, Tony shifted the drive of the conversation, looking for the 'right' appreciative question. These moments have been my strongest learning experience in these days because I perceived clearly the connection between conversation, thoughts, feelings and action style. I felt that this experience was shared also by the others new and old friends as an important difference from the experience of other projects. My feeling (and my hope) is that we are going to make a new experience and to build up a new kind of cooperation and friendship...learning to ask the right questions. And I realized also that this new path needs a lot of concentration, openness, strength, ethical consciousness and cooperative effort as a mutual help. But it needs also to enjoy ourselves, to smile, to be relaxed!

Inshallah!

Francesco

Example 2: Respecting different perspectives as a strength

In a PAAR approach to project management, the starting point to achieving the fundamental goal of sharing objectives and constructing a 'common language' amongst participants is to respect and valorise their different 'visions', expectations and communication styles. This 'diversity' is a rich resource for the working group, and therefore for the project itself. It is upon diversity – including inter-cultural diversity – that the identity of the group is built and a trust-based cooperation process takes root.

Simona interprets her most significant moment through a drawing that incorporates the key-words: the expectations of the various participants, the emotional perceptions felt during the meeting, and the decision-making process springing from a polyphonic vision of the project.

For Galia, it is an awareness of the respect for inter-cultural differences that proves to be a powerful catalyst that triggers an informed and aware 'engagement':

> My 'significant moment' happened during our third day of discussion. We had already had two intense days of working and I felt tired. The schedule of the day was to finalise the last frame of agreement on the activities of the project. Even though we had this very well designed plan for the day, the conversation was unfolding somehow unstructured or at least this is how I perceived it…. Francesco suggested that we go on with the discussion and the following topic I remember was 'participation' and Tony suggested that the participation is the basic principle of the project. I commented that we had to define what participation means because in Bulgaria non-participation was a good kind of participation in the Communist times and many Bulgarians tend to keep it. (Maybe it was my own resistance to participate in the project…). My memory was that Tony looked somehow confused, the group did not comment and we went on as if I had not said this. Later

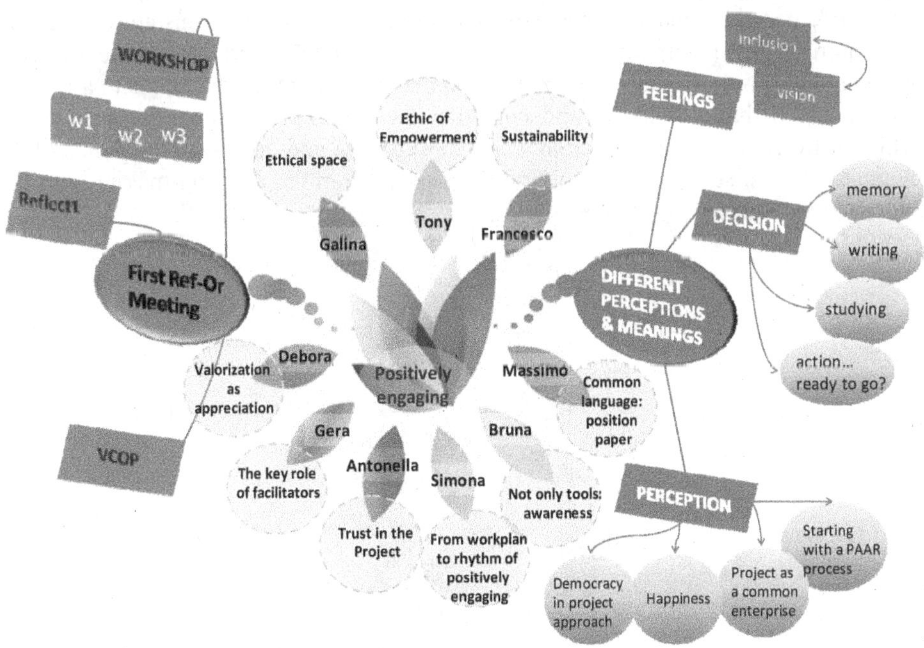

Figure 2. Respecting different perspectives as a strength.

though when Tony structured the discussion he asked: do we agree that the basis of the project is '**active participation**'?

This was the moment when I experienced something like a small wave of energy. It became very clear that unless a person wants to participate the project will fail. This simple frame made me feel free. Now, a couple of weeks after the moment passed, I realise that in that moment I obtained a small space to choose whether to participate or not. There was something in the group which made me feel this space. I did not feel pressed. It seems that it was important for me that my explanation about the non-participation as a cultural type of participation was heard and it changed the definition of the term 'participation' that we planned to use I the project into the term 'active participation'.

It was not very conscious what I experienced then but when I got back to Sofia and I told my colleagues about the project, my colleague shared that I was changed somehow, I was more enthusiastic.

This is my picture of a circle inside which you can see my small space of freedom, which I called very spontaneously 'degrees of freedom'. Why I used this statistical term – I have no idea.

Appreciatively

Galia

Example 3: Appreciating a different rhythm

Periodic meetings by consortium partners are key-milestones in European projects. An agenda based on goals to be achieved and scheduled slots/sessions are fundamental requirements underpinning each meeting. A PAAR approach to the project-management process requires less structured meetings in which the aim is to allow all participants to have their say and construct the group's identity together. This is achieved by valorising the different forms of expertise and different viewpoints of its members, and in so doing determining a slower pace in the decision-making process and often a re-scheduling of the agenda.

Figure 3. Appreciating a different rhythm.

In describing her most significant moment, one of the participants identified her awareness of the need for a different 'rhythm' in managing the meeting and decision-making process as being the turning-point that for her made it easier to engage.

Changing the rhythm, easing out

At the beginning

I felt riding a motor bike, riding fast, seeing fuzzy forms. My questions were: Am I going to lose time? How to get results as soon as possible?

Then, I start to slow down

I got off the motor bike. I looked around in search of something. My questions were: For the time being, why do not wait and see? New means of transportation? Which one? Where?

At the end

I found out a new – slower – means of transport; a new – slower - cruising speed; the pleasure of travelling; The pleasure of details; the pleasure of travelling and sharing discoveries…with new fellow travellers.

To summarise, in their role as facilitators of ITOs managed following a PAAR approach, project managers must be able to:

(1) constantly redefine the project boundaries and the roles played by the various actors involved;
(2) follow 'rhythms' and 'outcomes' of the decision-making process that might well be effective but may not always fit in with the established work plan;
(3) actively delegate the lead roles not just to the core partner or consortium partners but also to the enlarged partnership;
(4) propose new facilitation tools that, for example, enhance the sharing of positive stories and narratives;
(5) base the key strategy for the facilitation of knowledge flows and of the process of enhancing human resources and co-constructing both the project's decision-making process and its outcomes, on the group's periodic meetings and workshops; and
(6) propose new indicators and perspectives for analysis in assessing and evaluating the success of the project.

At the same time, a project such as Reflect-OR has management, execution and reporting rules that are strictly pre-defined and standard (Bienzle et al., 2010). It is clear, therefore, that in his or her facilitator role, the PAAR project manager must constantly seek to achieve a delicate balance between needs that may often appear dichotomous.

References

Bechky, B. (2006). Gaffers, golfers, and grips: Role-based coordination in temporary organizations. *Organization Science, 17,* 3–22.

Bienzle, H., Hedman, E., Kirtley, R., Purokuro, V., Rus, C., Wiesinger, S., & Wilen, E. (2010). *Survival kit. Managing multilateral projects in the lifelong learning programme.* Vienno, Germany: Die Berater.

Cooperrider, D., & Srivasta, S. (1987). Appreciative inquiry in organizational life. *Research in Organizational Change and Development, 1,* 129–169, http://www.stipes.com/aichap3.htm"http://www.stipes.com/aichap3.htm. Retrieved 26 February 2010.

Cooperrider, D., & Whitney, D. (2005). *Appreciative inquiry: A positive revolution in change.* San Francisco: Berrett-Koehler Publishers.

Engeström, Y., Miettinen, R. & Punamäki, R.L. (1999). *Perspectives in activity theory.* Cambridge: Cambridge University Press.

European Commission (2007). The European Research Area: New perspectives. Green Paper

Franz, H.W., & Sarcina, R., (2009). Building leadership in project and network management. A facilitator's tool set. Berlin, Heidelberg and New York: Springer.

Ghaye, T. (2008). *An introduction to participatory and appreciative action research (PAAR).* Gloucester: New Vista Publications.

Ghaye, T., Melander-Wikman, A., Kisare, M., Chambers, P., Bergmark, U., Kostenius, C., & Lillyman, S. (2008). Participatory and appreciative action and reflection (PAAR). Democratizing reflective practices. *Reflective Practice, 9*(4), 361–397.

Goodman, L.P., & Goodman, R.A. (1972). Theatre as a temporary system. *California Management Review, 40*(2), 103–108.

Goodman, L.P, & Goodman, R.A. (1976). Some management issues in temporary systems: A study of professional development and manpower – The theatre case. *Administrative Science Quarterly, 21,* 494–501.

Janowicz-Panjaitan, M., Bakker, R.M., & Kenis, P. (2009). Research on temporary organizations: The state of the art and distinct approaches towards temporariness. In P. Kenis, M. Janowicz-Panjaitan & M., Cambré (Eds.), *Temporary organizations. Prevalence, logic and effectiveness* (p. 56–85), Massachusetts: Edward Elgar Publishing.

Keith, P.M. (1978). Individual and organizational correlates of a temporary system. *The Journal of Applied Behavioral Science, 14*(2), 195–203.

Kenis, P., Janowicz-Panjaitan, M., & Cambré, M. (2009). *Temporary organizations. Prevalence, logic and effectiveness.* Massachussetts: Edward Elgar Publishing.

Midler, C. (1995). 'Projectification' of the firm: The Renault case. *Scandinavian Journal of Management, 11*(4), 363–375.

Moreley, E., & Silver, A. (1977). A film director's approach to managing creativity. *Harvard Business Review, 55*(2), 59–70.

Perrow, C.B. (1991). A society of organizations. *Theory and Society, 20*(6), 725–762.

Reynolds, M., & Vince, R. (2004). *Organizing reflection.* London: Ashgate.

Turner, J.R., & Muller, R. (2003). On the nature of the project as a temporary organisation. *International Journal of Project Management, 21,* 1–8.

Weick, K. (1974). Amendments to organizational theorizing. *The Academy of Management Journal, 17*(3), 487–502.

Whiltey, R. (2006). Project-based firms: The new organizational form or variations on a theme?, *Industrial and Corporate Change, 15*(1), 77–99.

Co-constructing an appreciative and collective eye: appreciative reflection in action in lifelong career guidance

Simona Marchi

Department of Economics, 'Sapienza' University of Rome, Rome, Italy and Reflective Learning Italy, Rome, Italy

> That which has been given becomes a starting point for a quest, a starting point for a task that is by no means one of ownership. It is a task, rather, that revolves around a desire that will continue to learn that each of its forms of expression is a disappointment. (De Certeau, 2010, p. 7)

This is not a paper, it is a space where the experiences of the participants in the Reflect-OR project can be read directly. As a selection, albeit an agreed one, it is by definition a biased product and is influenced by the point of view of the person who, in one way or another, has organised it as a text. If we set out the criterion adopted, the process can be seen to be less partial. Of the many choices available, I preferred a narration/listening structure focusing on the concept of appreciative reflection. Taking this as my starting point, I adopted a second criterion: to include the greatest possible variability in the positions expressed on this subject. The third criterion was to group these in three thematic areas:

(1) developing a collective and participatory appreciative memory;
(2) discovering the richness and strength of the group to foster well-being in work; and
(3) adopting the organisation's viewpoint to move on from a conflictual approach to change.

These are the crucial issues on the road to developing an appreciative eye in the Reflect-OR project. The voices speaking here can be read as reflections on appreciative reflection in action.

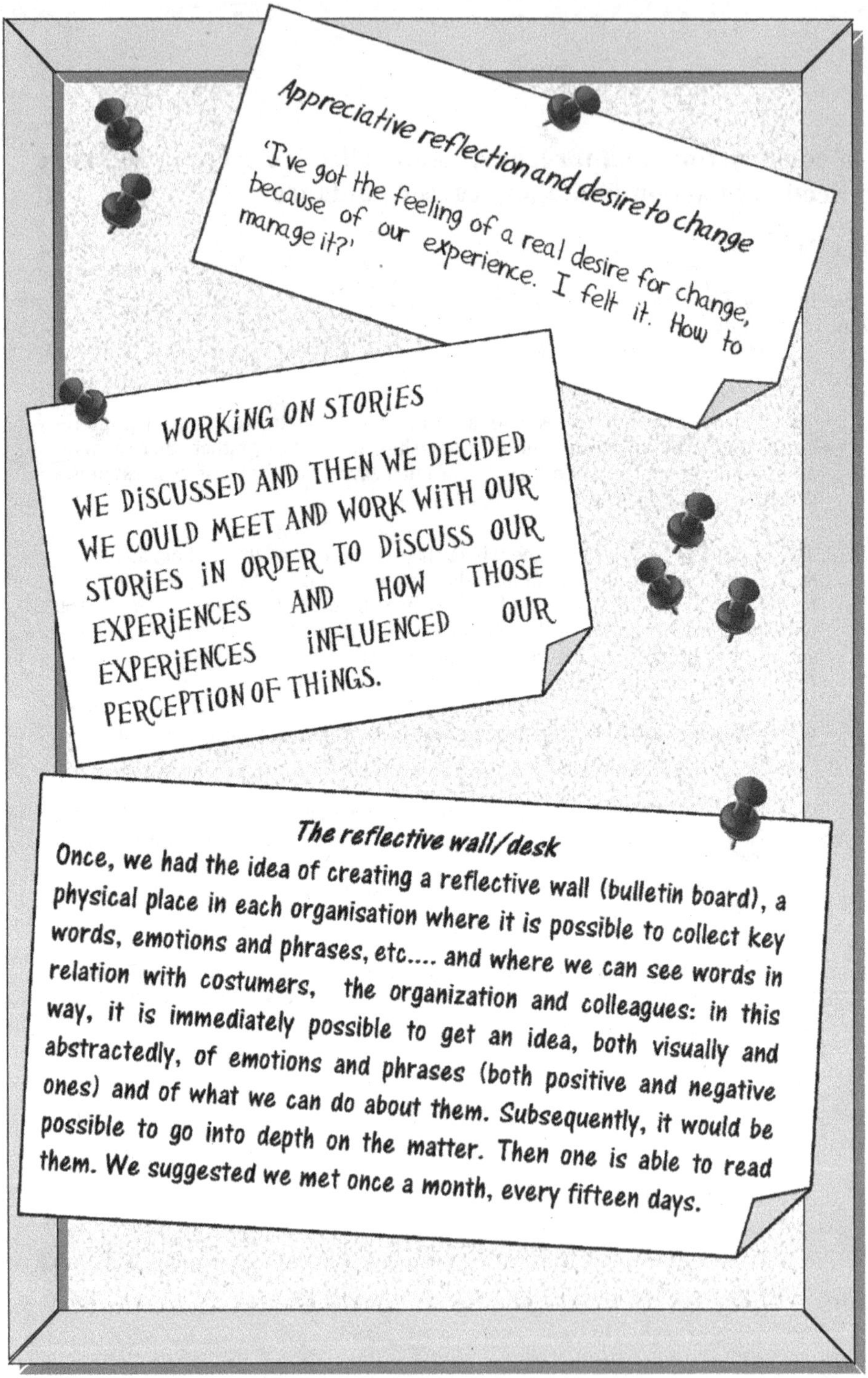
Appreciative reflection and desire to change
'I've got the feeling of a real desire for change, because of our experience. I felt it. How to manage it?'
WORKING ON STORIES
WE DISCUSSED AND THEN WE DECIDED WE COULD MEET AND WORK WITH OUR STORIES IN ORDER TO DISCUSS OUR EXPERIENCES AND HOW THOSE EXPERIENCES INFLUENCED OUR PERCEPTION OF THINGS.
The reflective wall/desk
Once, we had the idea of creating a reflective wall (bulletin board), a physical place in each organisation where it is possible to collect key words, emotions and phrases, etc.... and where we can see words in relation with costumers, the organization and colleagues: in this way, it is immediately possible to get an idea, both visually and abstractedly, of emotions and phrases (both positive and negative ones) and of what we can do about them. Subsequently, it would be possible to go into depth on the matter. Then one is able to read them. We suggested we met once a month, every fifteen days.

Introduction

In the Italian lifelong career guidance (LLCG) context, the Reflect-OR project presented four challenges.

The first challenge regarded the specific nature of the project as part of the Leonardo da Vinci Transfer of Innovation (TOI). This required us to focus on the type of innovation to be transferred. The transfer was linked, in this case, to the experience gained in a previous European project (Reflect) and the identification of transfer methods and channels. All of this translated into a multi-faceted and experience-based learning pathway.

The second challenge was linked to the type of innovation to be transferred. In our case, this was represented by the use of a specific methodological approach: reflective practice (Stroobants, Chamber, & Clark, 2007). Throughout the project, as participants and facilitators, we sought to identify the best ways to transfer a methodological approach, i.e., reflective practice. Here, the methodology being transferred was learnt using that same methodology in what could be described as an on-going feedback process. The methodological approach therefore was at one and the same time the means and the end of the transfer.

The third challenge was that within this approach we introduced a further innovation. In the Reflect project, the reflective practice revolved around critical reflection and the development of learning processes and actions based on the reflections arising from critical incidents, usually identified as negative events. In the Reflect-OR project, on the other hand, we focused on appreciative reflection; namely, the development of action and learning processes based on valuing and building upon what works, what makes us feel good, what we perceive as positive, and what gives us a sense of strength and well-being in the work we do.

The fourth challenge lay in the fact that appreciative reflection touches upon the way that participants, each belonging to their own organisational culture, perceive the relationship between reflection, action and change. This challenge is linked to the previous ones and is a response to this question: 'How can we develop an appreciative reflection in organisational contexts where the dynamics of change are rarely associated with individual learning and organisational processes and often associated with conflict management methods and processes generated by critical or troubled situations?'

In this paper we will describe the tensions, apparent contradictions, difficulties and opportunities encountered in relation to the development of the 'appreciative eye'.

1. Appreciating our appreciativity

The term 'appreciative' has at least three meanings in the literature on organisational learning: First: as Geoffrey Vickers (1968) wrote: 'Appreciative systems are a culture's system of values, beliefs, and expectations that guide perception and action'. Appreciative systems reside in a readiness to see and value and respond in a certain situation in a certain way. This understanding of 'appreciative' is linked to assessment processes and self-reinforcing systems (Barrett, 1995). From this perspective, appreciative systems influence the way we perceive and act with respect to new experience but at the same time are changed by that experience.

Second, Schön (1983) mentioned that practitioners bring certain 'constants to their reflection-in-action'. They provide the necessary boundaries for most reflective practice. These constants are:

- the media, languages and repertoires they use to describe reality;
- the appreciative systems they bring to problem setting, to the evaluation of inquiry and to reflective conversation;
- the overarching theories by which they make sense of phenomena; and
- the role frames within which they set their tasks and through which they bind their institutional settings. (p. 270)

In this case, the appreciative system is a necessary pre-condition for reflection-in-action:

> Constancy of appreciative system is an essential condition for reflection-in-action. It is what makes possible the initial framing of the problematic situation, and it is also what permits the inquirer to re-appreciate the situation in the light of its back-talk, and it allows the inquirer to tell when he is finished. (Schön, 1983, p. 272)

Schön's perspective is more situational and is linked to the 'ethic of enquiry' concept, whereby an actor acts in fluctuating situations. Appreciative systems make it possible to link subjective knowledge to explicit knowledge and combine the learning and knowing perspectives. Appreciative systems are not set in stone, and indeed may change from one practitioner to another, and over time. They provide a fairly robust and stable reference system so that in the reflective process individual practitioners may feel at ease in opening up to discussion the theories and mental structures they use in their professional practices.

The third meaning is related to the word 'appreciate': to value what is best about a human system; to recognise the best qualities in people and in the world around us; to affirm past and present points of strength, success and potential; to perceive the things that give us energy, health, vitality and a positive outlook; to increase in value, to give value. In this case, the concept of appreciate refers to the system's ability to grasp, value and build upon positive potential. It refers to the ability to see beyond obstacles, problems and limitations and to generate hope in the human capacity to achieve potential (Barrett, 1995).

This way of conceiving appreciativity requires us to develop an appreciative intelligence (Thatchenkery, 2005; Thatchenkery & Metzker, 2006, Thatchenkery & Chowdhry, 2007). This is composed of three elements:

(1) the ability to appreciate the positive,
(2) the ability to re-frame experiences; and
(3) the ability to see how the future unfolds from aspects of the positive present:

> Because the people we interviewed could re-frame, appreciate the positive and see how the future could unfold from the present, they could see how their end goal was possible to accomplish. Thus, they were willing to persist and to believe that their own actions and abilities would take them to a successful conclusion. Because they could envision the way a positive future could unfold from the present, they could deal with the uncertainty that often accompanies a new venture or a crisis. They exhibited irrepressible resilience, the ability to bounce back from a difficult situation, as the result of re-framing, seeing what was positive in the situation, and understanding that a better future could come about despite a crisis or setback. (Thatchenkery & Metzker 2006, pp. 15–16)

Appreciative reflection is often contrasted with critical reflection. The former is associated with a more positive, creative and generative thinking, while the second is often understood as being focused solely on problems – a deficit-based approach to problem-solving. Appreciative reflection (Ghaye & Marchi, 2011) is based on the development of an appreciative eye (Ghaye, 2008) and starts from the assumption that something, somewhere is working well in the organisation. The reflection process begins, therefore, with a focusing on the characteristics and dynamics seen in the organisation and/or system when they are working well.

As Barrett (1995) wrote:

> the art of appreciation is the art of discovering and valuing those factors that give life to the organisation, of identifying what is best in the current organisation. Appreciation involves the investment of emotional and cognitive energy to create a positive image of a desired future. (p. 40)

This happens through a process that Senge calls 'generative conversation' starting from the best of 'what is' and moving on to envisioning 'what might be'.

Over and above the dichotomisations that in practice are hardly ever backed up by empirical evidence, we believe that the shift from critical to appreciative reflection is, in conceptual terms, highly significant. Senge (1990) states that the failure to understand system dynamics can lead us into 'cycles of blaming and self-defense: the enemy is always out there, and problems are always caused by someone else' (Senge, 1990, p. 231). The risk is that a problem-oriented reflection will generate a problem-oriented framing of the situation and a problem-oriented language.

The focus inevitably shifts to critical and unexpected events perceived as negative. Organisations and practitioners become, in most cases, unable to develop a positive reflection on the strong points and potential of individuals and of the system as a whole. This generates a defence mechanism that makes it difficult to create relations of trust and blocks individual, group and organisational learning processes.

According to Barrett (1995) the appreciative approach gives rise to generative learning: 'appreciative learning cultures nurture innovative thinking by fostering an affirmative focus, expansive thinking, a generative sense of meaning, and creating collaborative systems' (p. 42). This is based on the creation of the necessary conditions for the development of specific competences:

- the ability to focus on what was successful in the past for organisations and individuals and what is going well in the present (*affirmative competence*);
- the ability to expand the sense of what is possible, to frame problems even in unfamiliar settings, to redefine and go beyond the boundaries of one's own experience (*expansive competence*);
- the ability to construct a feedback system in which it is possible to highlight the way in which the contribution of each participant can make a difference, to convey a sense of progress in which each participant can recognise that they have made a significant contribution (*generative competence*); and
- the ability to establish a collaborative dialogue between participants with a view to transforming systems, creating a positive space for dialogue and inquiry, exchanges of views and mutual help, that are open to different voices and perspectives; spaces, forums to think together creatively to generate future visions (*collaborative competence*).

The PAAR approach used in the Reflect-OR project continues to use critical reflection as an analysis method to build a sense of the reality and characteristics of the context:

> […] the action research process often starts with an individual practitioner reflecting on an aspect of their work and looking for areas where changes might be made. The focus of the action is often *framed* as a problem or a concern. This conception of action research is, therefore, about reducing perplexity and discomfort, with a change process as *fixing* and getting rid of problems. Because of this, some forms of action research can be associated with deficit-based discourses. (Ghaye, 2008, p. 5, emphasis in original)

At the same time, however, it does not consider critical reflection as the only mode of reflection on which action and change decisions are based. It is set within an appreciative approach that tends to focus on successes, strong points, on what has gone and is going well, and that tends to accentuate a positive way to look problems 'within a creative and appreciative frame and with a critical spirit' (Ghaye et al., 2008, p. 362).

In this sense, PAAR can provide a good opportunity to consider both aspects, since it does not entail diverting the eye from the problems. At the same time:

> […] this means that achieving and moving forward does not have to be only about getting rid of what we don't want, namely problems. Conversations and actions do not have to be only about 'fixing' things that are going less well, less than we had hoped for or expected. PAAR does not perpetuate the belief that weaknesses can, indeed, simply be fixed. PAAR requires a major shift in our mindset, away from reflective practices being only about problem finding, problem solving and about getting rid of 'unwanted' aspects of current practice, away from confessional tales and towards conversations about success, about understanding why particular aspects of our work are indeed successful, and how these joyful and celebratory aspects of practice can be further amplified and made more consistent. First and foremost it is about identifying and playing to our strengths (Ghaye et al., 2008, p. 362).

Very briefly, our field of practice seems to be characterised by a continuum that ranges from critical to appreciative reflection. Within this continuum, we find a constellation of extremely interesting contributions, ideas and practices that present different characteristics depending on which elements are emphasised.

In the Reflect-OR project, this continuum emerged in all its nuances. In this paper we shall describe these nuances and try to place readers in a position to visualise the waves of reflection and emotion. We shall try to move forward in the reflection by imagining possible responses to the provocative questions that emerged with respect to each issue covered and set out at the end of each section.

2. Developing a participatory and collective appreciative memory

Developing the ability to remember, memorise, value and share all the things in our work that have gone and are going well, the things that plan out and make us feel good, is neither an immediate nor a simple matter. Each of these processes – remembering, memorising, valuing and sharing positive aspects – requires a series of intentional actions and situation-related social skills. These cannot be taken for granted and require a confidence-building effort by participants and a specific learning process.

The difficulty of remembering the good things

> I think the appreciative method is important to keep in mind. But the thing that has always driven me to change and improve is the critical method. I have always picked

myself up – stronger and with more enthusiasm – from negative experiences, mistakes, dissatisfactions, falls. I forget the good things. I don't retain positive achievements in my memory. In fact, I couldn't find any significant positive situations to remember and to talk about. Negative experiences enrich me and I find it easy to remember them. The situations that come to mind are the negative ones that have led me to improve. I struggle, though, to remember good times and periods, although there certainly must have been lots of them. But they don't come to mind. I don't remember them. (CIOFS practitioner)

The difficulty of speaking about our successes

At the start the difficulty was to speak about our successes, so positive experiences and change. Another difficulty is the fear of exposing yourself: maybe people are afraid to speak up.... I was struck by a colleague who hadn't said anything until that point and then told us about her positive experience. I find this sort of exchange amongst colleagues very enriching. (COL practitioner)

The need to develop an oral tradition based on appreciativity

It is important, in my view, to insist on this thing – this appreciativity – which at the outset I found a bit irritating. Then I thought about it and said to myself that maybe it was no mere chance that I found it tiresome. That's because it breaks down the oral tradition you find in the COLs, where we all tell each other negative stories, even though we have an excellent ability to value and appreciate our users. In my opinion this has an impact on what we mean by 'group'. The COL group already exists but we need a change in the oral tradition, because the habit is to tell each other stories that are not positive'. (COL task force)

Infinite memories

For me, a significant moment is one where an encounter and/or a fact so loaded with feeling and true, rich communication occurs that it gives rise to a reflection mechanism and a desire to dig more deeply. I mean, a personal decision to be 100% present. It's a long phrase, maybe, but I can identify with this definition. So I tried to go over in my mind the training days we had in June.... From images I need to move on to gestures, words, silences, sounds and even moments. I need to work.

I put myself into this mindset and these are the words that appeared: remember, open up to new experience, reflect, relive with new eyes, collect myself, gather, and again, remember, for another experience of sharing and a new interaction and new encounter. And remember yet again. Because if I share, if I enter into an interaction and encounter mechanism, then other memories spring up. Therefore infinite memories. I start from a memory to arrive at another moment of the memory. I start from a memory. There's the word 'heart' in remembering...putting something into your heart. Open up, relive with new eyes, collect myself, gather, enter into the story. I mustn't lose track of the story while I'm following this pathway. I need to feel free and without constraints, then I need to order the experiences I have lived through to start over again from the memory. My experience has been something like this. (CIOFS practitioner)

From the voices of our participants we can see that the act of remembering, for the individual, corresponds to a memory reactualisation process that takes place with the help of a group, which can be large or small. This involves two aspects: the past is not 'stored away', it is not filed away once and for all. Rather, it is found again and reconstructed on the basis of the present, in forms that are often unpredictable and unprecedented, depending on the type of group within which this reconstruction process is taking place. The function of the group comes to be of fundamental importance in this reconstruction since it aids the process of individual 'reprocessing' and interpretation through the construction of a collective memory.

Developing a collective appreciative memory in the Reflect-OR project meant embarking on a reflective learning process within which each individual identified a set of significant events relating to their professional practices, as experienced through their relationship with their clients, the organisation and their colleagues. They began to reconstruct the memory itself through the storytelling technique in order to build on the positive aspects and those which, from various points of view, worked well. This process developed within a relational dynamic in which participants mutually took on the role of active-activating witnesses of the appreciative memory, not, therefore, of the individual past as such, but of its reconstruction in a collective, positive light. This was done through a process of ethical appreciative inquiry (Ghaye & Marchi, 2011).

Provocative questions

- How does this appreciative reflective approach fit in with our day-to-day practices?
- To what extent are we capable of taking forward this concept of an appreciative eye and an appreciative memory?
- What will happen to our appreciative memory when the project ends?

3. Discovering the richness and strength of the group to foster well-being in work

The main function of the group in the Reflect-OR project was to encourage the transition from an individual to a collective dimension of reflection. This transition, which was structured as a project-long process, envisaged a double level of action and reflection: the reconstruction and reactualisation of individual experiences and the sharing of those experiences through the storytelling tool; their reformulation based on valuing and appreciating the positive aspects.

The construction of bonds of trust and ethical relations between the group members was fundamental to this double level of re-framing. It enabled participants to overcome the fear of speaking up and of feeling exposed to others' judgement. It also paved the way to develop an awareness of how important the role of the other is in formulating different ways to remember, read and perceive situations and creative ways to imagine solutions and operational proposals for improvement.

Discovering the richness of colleagues

> What struck me was the richness of my colleagues – that's something I've brought away with me from this experience. The strength to move on from all that talk of demands or dependency and to try to actually get things moving. So this opportunity could help us to change things both in and about the organisation. (COL task force)

The strength of the group

The depth that we were able to achieve was very interesting for me. To start with, because we managed to 'read' the organisation starting from events and individual ways of feeling. The difficulty of being, of being present, with a sense of energy, presence, affectionate kindness, responsibility. Some colleagues have 'disinvested' in their work because they have invested in their private lives and they can't maintain those two levels of energy. This group too has been very conflictual in the past. But one colleague told the story of the transition they had made: from a conflictual stance to recognising our value as a group and the strength that that gives you and the fact that over time all of this has settled, been laid down, and enabled us to find solutions. I heard them say that they were working well, they gave examples of tasks performed well. They're satisfied with their work and their emotional relationships. For me, that was astonishing. (COL task force)

The need to invest more in the group

At a certain point we became aware that we were working on a double level. While we're more mature in understanding, in trying to understand why there's no communication with the hierarchical organisation, we noticed that we find it harder to work, discuss and tackle things with the colleagues we work with on a day-to-day basis. Although not everybody felt this way. The group was split. Some people wanted immediate solutions, others said that this talk about methodology might be a useful tool to address these issues, while others still just came to a halt and said they had done all they could. (COL task force)

The right dimension for the group

This method, using small groups, seems to work. It seemed to me (there were six of us) that it could be a way to get to know different colleagues in a different way, without the formal bureaucratic dimension that a large group can have. You can hear someone's point of view, get to know them better, get to know them in more depth. I found that the small group is less likely to get side-tracked – the dialogue and exchange of views is frequent and direct. It's more direct.

In fact, when we discussed it amongst ourselves, we felt that next time we meet we should keep to the same group – because we like this group. We'd like it to be us, again. We'd like to get used to working and discussing things together. I find it really interesting. It establishes a different climate from what you'd find in a formal work meeting. It adds emotional and relationship elements to the goals. Doing things together. There wasn't a big distinction between facilitator and facilitated. It didn't even seem that there *was* a facilitator because we were all taking part in the same way. It was natural. Maybe in larger groups things change and it's more difficult to manage. We didn't record the sessions and maybe that too helped us to be more spontaneous. (COL task force)

The group as a factor in working and organisational well-being

I could also see the differences between groups. In another group, there was one person in particular who was much more resistant to change, to thinking about a positive experience and not approaching everything in terms of 'them and us' (i.e., in contraposition to the organisation). One colleague, on the other hand, underscored the aspect of 'us', as a working group.

Some interesting metaphors emerged. One was the organisation as a mother who needs to protect and support you, and so the extent to which we too place ourselves in this relationship of dependency on this mother that needs to give and do everything for us,

> while we ourselves become passive with respect to this situation. Here too, one colleague had something very interesting to say because he stepped outside this mindset. He underlined this dimension of the group as a group of adults trying to tackle the organisation's difficulties, because there's an awareness that the basis for all of this is satisfaction, well-being, the fact that we can feel pleased to come into work. (COL task force)

During the project's life cycle, the way of perceiving the group's function and the approach used were not constant. Individual stories, and those of the reference organisations, generated different waves of participation and sharing that produced varied and various meanings and attitudes. The main signals of this variability – signals that are extremely useful to the facilitators in their reflections – were presence and participation in meetings, the swings between critical/conflictual mode and an appreciative way to manage situations. This oscillation gave rise to generative reflections that focused primarily on the relationship between practitioners and organisation.

Provocative questions

- When will we have another chance to meet and speak in this way? And what exactly is 'this way'?
- What has changed in our way of being together, from when we started up until now?
- In what way was Reflect-OR useful with respect to our professional practices with colleagues, customers and organisations? How, and to what extent, did this take root?

4. Stand in the organisation's shoes to try to move on from an approach based on conflict

Reflection on relationships with the organisation was one of the hottest topics, for various reasons, within the different groups of project participants. During the project, the COL organisation underwent two management changes, while CIOFS was reformulating its service offering in light of legislative changes concerning vocational training. All of this should be considered against a background of economic crisis and rising unemployment for all age groups, educational qualifications and economic sectors. In this situation, reflection on the relationship with the organisation was structured, over time, through a system of contraposition involving three actors: 'I' (individual/practitioner), 'us' (group of practitioners) and 'them' (organisation – central administration or line manager).

With full respect for this way of perceiving relationships with the organisation, we worked on this axis of reflection by seeking to identify positive significant events in order to understand better their generative aspects and the best conditions to strengthen and reproduce them. This enabled us – often but not always – to blur and make more fluid the boundaries between the three actors (I, us, them) in an attempt to establish which conditions would develop an appreciative working environment.

Surgery or homeopathy?

> One metaphor to sum up the relationship currently existing between Reflect-OR and practitioners' problems would be what's happening now in medicine between surgery

and homeopathy. There's a widespread malaise afflicting us, in that we don't have responses from the people who should be providing those responses (them). But we ourselves aren't able to formulate the questions. We continue to be few in number, and overwhelmed by too much work. The general feeling, for different reasons, is that we need a figure to restore 'legality', in an ethical sense, at least. A blend of competent director, reflective manager…surgery, in short.

All of this notwithstanding, some aliens (us), who take part in mysterious meetings, propose that we should try to talk about problems through the lens of appreciative reflective practice (or something similar): a slow and difficult process, that involves discussion and debate and maybe even some conflict, and works over the longer term on a basis of trust. But when it works, things go better, they move forward. Homeopathy, or any treatment discipline that intends to work with the person rather than the symptom. If we want to promote homeopathy, i.e., reflectiveness, we must not turn it into a parallel track to the debates currently taking place. We must, rather, promote it, including on questions concerning our day-to-day working life. (COL task force)

Methodology as a resource for change

Our organisation has difficulty governing processes. The resources that are activated all fall on our fragile shoulders. Sometimes I'd like to 'close the factory gates' and protest, at other times I think we're offering a service that we can't just shut down. We don't slow down the pace of work. The thing that I feel is very positive is that in midst of this feeling of distress we saw this Reflect-OR experience as a great resource. It's a sign that in some way this opportunity for reflection is very important to us. The expectation is to understand that this reflection can help us reach agreed decisions that can also be very demanding for us. (COL task force)

Taking the organisation's point of view

On the question of 'us' practitioners versus 'them' organisation we finally understood that we were also curious to get to know them (the organisational and administrative staff) and to understand why, in effect, they couldn't respond to our needs. Then we started working almost empathetically, saying, but if I were in their shoes and nearly every morning I get 60 phone calls, each one of them urgent. (COL task force)

Towards activating an appreciative working environment

A colleague came out with a story about difficulties, a failure with a user. But what happened, and the thing that I liked, was the relationship within the group. Very emotional. Our colleagues turned this story about problems and difficulties into something positive through emotion and their appreciation of the positive things this person had done. From 'me with the user' the conversation was changed into 'us, what we can say, what we can do, what we do'. And by going through these stages the conversation was shifted from 'us to the organisation' and so to 'them'.

On this too, however, we were able in my opinion to work in a different way, because this emotional, affectionate, positive, empathetic dimension had been activated. The idea was that we are not an easy group to manage, and to put ourselves in the organisation's shoes. We asked ourselves: who knows what they think about this? Who knows what they're going through? With all these questions, not demands – questions posed through a desire for more knowledge. So we'd like to know what their work successes are. What exactly is a success for them? When they manage to meet one of our requests, or when they get us out from under their feet…or what? (COL task force)

The role of the group in changing the mutual 'us-them' definition

> This is the first time that, speaking with my colleagues, I've felt that we've managed to move away from that 'us-them' position, to a reflection on 'who knows what they think of us', what they've got to say. Individually you can make this shift, but it's in the group dimension that it doesn't happen, that an explosive conflictual dynamic takes root. The feeling that we are 'us' often means feeling that we're 'us against'. Maybe the fact that we were a small group helped…. I don't know'. (task force)

The discussion of the organisation brought out very clearly the interweaving – which can be something of a dilemma – between the different systems of rules and values with respect to which practitioners make their decisions for action and the ethical question becomes crucial. This generally emerged as a need 'not to betray the trust' of certain people in specific situations/contexts. If we try to name the different systems of rules with respect to the way in which the ethical question is posed, the following ethical dimensions emerged:

- ethics of the relationship with users/clients: do not betray their trust with regard to their expectations of a welcome, reception, a listening ear and guidance/support;
- ethics of the relationship with colleagues: do not betray their trust with regard to their expectations of understanding, capability, responsibility, acknowledgement;
- ethics of labour relations: do not betray trust with regard to expectations of the protection of the rights and duties of practitioners working in a given area of practice;
- ethics of relations with the local area: do not betray trust with regard to expectations as to the development of the guidance, support and employment insertion and inclusion service for users/clients;
- ethics of the relationship with the organisation: do not betray trust with regard to expectations of continuity, quality and performance in work; and
- ethics of the Reflect-OR project: do not betray trust with regard to the expectations of the project group and the participants and goals of the project itself.

In this complex system of situation-based ethics two aspects can be highlighted: the difficulty of defining the reciprocity of ethical questions with regard to the various contexts and interlocutors, which means that the ethical question is often, though not always, posed as being mainly 'under the charge of' a given person. In relations with the organisation, the question of ethics constantly places relationships with other systems of situation-based ethics in question and renders them spurious.

Appreciative reflection has set something in motion with respect to these systems. First of all, it has made it possible for another way of conceiving relationships with the organisation to be developed and accepted, one based more on a logic of 'do with' than 'manage without'. It has paved the way for a reflection on the dynamics of change that are not focused on the us-them conflict, by moving from a logic of contraposition to one of agreement and the sharing of responsibility and accountability. All this has given rise to decision-making micro-processes and actions that will foster greater reciprocity within and between the different systems of situation-based ethics.

This process of reactivating different systems of situation-based ethics could be termed *ethical constructionism*, based on a more generative and transformative concept of constructionist ethics in which ethical decision-making places ethical decisions within the interaction between individuals. But there is more. COL and CIOFS practitioners influence and are influenced by clients, events and social realities that inform professional action, including ethical systems and dilemmas, laws, and community standards. From an appreciative reflection perspective, ethical systems are more responsive to context, are culturally dependent, are always local and are interconnected.

Provocative questions

- Did Reflect-OR fuel our motivation and help us to support the organisation when it was in trouble? When did we realise this?
- Is there a risk with appreciative reflection that a state of affairs that isn't working will be kept going by this very process of fuelling our motivation (or empowerment), even when the organisation is absent or in a crisis situation? How and when did we perceive this risk?
- Is there a risk that appreciative learning could make us become parties to an organisation's inefficiencies? How and when did we perceive this risk?

5. Towards an appreciative reflection: self-assessment reflections

This section brings together a selection of reflections by COL and CIOFS practitioners with respect to their experience in the Reflect-OR project and most notably with respect to the use of an approach based on appreciative reflection.

Developing the ability to take a longer view

> I decided to choose some photos to visualise and then say something about them. This is a photo I took this winter; for me it represents the effort to accustom our eyes to taking a longer view. This comes into my mind every summer because in the winter I'm in the office and what I see is the wall. In the summer, on the other hand, it's as though I get back this desire to accustom my eyes to look farther...and that's a real rest for the eyes.
>
> In some way, we need this ability to view things at a distance. Bringing them into focus but also looking farther away, there is – or can be – a different horizon. This has been useful to me in tackling this job.... Taking a longer view also means not letting difficulties or the tiredness of the moment stop you, but trying to understand the positive aspects of our experience. I managed to do this thanks to the people I've had discussions or compared myself with. Even when I saw that there was this informal atmosphere and a real enjoyment of being together, of doing things differently. Then I took another photo, this one of the mountain-climber, because it shows real effort and exertion.
>
> It's as though you had to keep climbing a mountain while at the same time realising that the view all around you is beautiful, and knowing that once you get to the top you'll be able to see those marvellous vistas. But when you're actually climbing, it's nothing but sheer effort. (CIOFS task force)

Banqueting together. Offering ourselves to each other, enjoying exchanges of viewpoints and finding out about each others' experiences

I found this picture, 'Citizens' wedding feast'. The reason I chose this has something to do with my background. I found many personal things in this picture. I use it to describe those sensations of satisfaction, a full tummy, in relation to our meetings together. They gave me the impression of a table laid for a feast. Of being invited to a wedding. A big table to which everyone brought their experience, themselves – as though they were food (spicy, savoury, sweet, bitter). I felt like a guest at this table – invited to taste and to offer something of myself, my experience, my voice.

I don't want to be too rhetorical or pedantic, but that way of being together, of sharing as though we were at a table where everyone was free to help themselves – in a good-mannered, pleasurable way – to the experiences recounted by the others, was so pleasant; you could tell they were authentic testimonies – it made me feel well and *be* well. I almost had the feeling of actually being full – so much so that I had the idea of depicting it through a picture of a table set for a meal.

I don't often experience this way of working, sadly, not this ability and freedom to share experiences. I find that this way of being together, of feasting together, which is important to me, with enjoyment, creativity, colour, the taste for hearing of others' experiences, is a key sharing experience. The climate at work is different. You share, you create, you enjoy yourself, you practise, you work. These are my ways of being well when I'm at work and of experiencing my working life in a positive way. (CIOFS task force)

Discovering that you've left a positive mark to renew and improve your efforts

The critical moment makes you feel a sense of failure (not succeeding in doing things). But we need to know that something else is happening, there are lots of events that make you feel good, that make you feel that what you're doing isn't useless. This type of reflection is both different and positive. You discover that you've left your mark (emotions, words, feelings). Taking all this on board renews your sense of commitment, translates it into life, enthusiasm, in yourself and in others, and enables you to go on, to improve yourself and the quality of the work you're doing. CIOFS task force)

Appreciative reflection in day-to-day working practice: do we want to introduce moments for reflection?

We had a critical event and it was marvellous to hear a colleague say, 'Do we want to introduce a time-out for reflection?' So we were able to think positively about tackling the problem and take positive steps to find solutions. It was wonderful. It's a confirmation that this thing has been set in motion – it's working. And you know that I was the very one who initially had doubts and resisted the idea. But now…. (COL task force)

Seeing things with a different eye

Personally, the thing that struck me was re-reading my notes. At the end I read them through again and I noticed that those strings of words I had written actually sketched out a pathway that closely reflected the pathway of the attitude I'd taken to this project. Since I started here my approach had been that I was more likely to speak about the negative things. And yet now I see things with another eye – a different eye. The things that emerged followed this same type of pathway and maybe at the end what I wished for was: to invent something, whatever we needed in order to go ahead. (COL task force)

Seeing people happy

> What I liked so much was to see people happy, see them breathe. There was room to breathe, with the others and with the outside world. And it's a method that doesn't stop within the four walls of the office – it can be transferred to other areas of your life. (CIOFS task force)

Letting go of stereotypes and prejudices

> In appreciative reflection I caught a glimpse of an instrument to open up the discussion with 'others', to develop an ability to interact in groups with fewer prejudices, without developing stereotypes. We can work on ourselves, on our internal conflicts, ideological perceptions, resistances. This approach should be used much more widely. (COL task force)

Transforming awareness into competence

> We'd like to be competent. We'd like to see this awareness of the method become a competence. (COL task force)

Concluding notes

This is just the first stage. It lasted two years and was itself packed with first stages. The first stage establishes a sort of punctuation. There are full stops and commas: noteworthy moments that structure time and establish a rhythm. Something happens that turns experience as we have understood it upside down and forces us to reformulate it. Something happens that surprises us and imposes a beginning and an end. Place, like a departure, makes the itinerary possible, it makes the follow-up possible, just like the sensation we have had in reading this chapter. But we cannot stand still at these starting points, get settled there, and lead the experience back to one of these moments. Each time the participants felt this temptation strongly during the project, their disappointment too was strong. There is a relationship between how much it is possible to draw from these moments and how much they still require of us. We are on our way.

Notes on contributor

Simona Marchi has been a researcher in the sociology of organizations, work, professions and innovation at the faculty of statistics, 'Sapienza' University of Rome, Italy, since 2001. Simona has a bachelor's degree in statistics, demographic and social sciences and a specialization in methods and techniques for social research. She has authored chapters on research methods, reflective learning and learning using Web 2.0 resources in Italian and international journals. These include: *Participatory and Appreciative Action and Reflection in Adult Learning* (IGI Global 2011) and *Participation and appreciativity in reflective learning* (2008, Formazione and Cambiamento). In 2008 she became president of Reflective Learning – Italy, www.reflectivelearning.it.

References

Barrett, F.J. (1995). Creating appreciative learning cultures. *Organizational Dynamics, 24*(2), 36–49.

Ghaye, T. (2008). *An introduction to participatory and appreciative action research (PAAR).* Gloucester: New Vista Publications.

Ghaye, T., & Marchi, S. (2011). *Appreciative reflection: How to feel positive and do good work.* Gloucester: New Vista Publications.

Ghaye, T., Melander-Wikman, A., Kisare, M., Chambers, P., Bergmark, U., Kostenius, C., & Lillyman, S. (2008). Participatory and appreciative action and reflection (PAAR) – Democratizing reflective practices. *Reflective Practice, 9*(4), 361–397.

Schön, D. (1983). *The reflective practitioner. How professionals think in action.* New York: Basic Books.

Senge, P.M. 1990. *The fifth discipline: The art and practice of the learning organization.* New York: Doubleday Currency.

Stroobants, H., Chambers, P., & Clarke, B. (Eds.). (2007). *Reflective journeys. A fieldbook for facilitating life-long learning in vocational education and training.* Leuven: Acco.

Thatchenkery, T. (2005). *Appreciative sharing of knowledge: Leveraging knowledge management for strategic change.* Ohio, Chagrin Falls: Taos Institute Publication.

Thatchenkery, T., & Chowdhry, D. (2007). *Appreciative inquiry and knowledge management: A social constructionist perspective.* Cheltenham: Edward Elgar.

Thatchenkery, T., & Metzker, C. (2006). *Appreciative intelligence: Seeing the mighty in the acorn.* San Francisco: Berrett-Koehler Publishers.

Vickers, G. (1968). *Values, systems and social processes.* Middlesex: Pelican Books.

Opening PAAR spaces in Bulgaria: reflective accounts

Galina Markova[a], Haralan Alexandrov[a], Nadejda Angelova[b] and Silviya Yordanova[b]

[a]*Education Management, New Bulgarian University, Sofia, Bulgaria;* [b]*JobTiger, Sofia, Bulgaria*

This text is a reflection on the process of opening participative appreciative action and reflection (PAAR) spaces in the Bulgarian context of career counseling within the project Reflect-OR. The authors – career counselors and university educators and researchers – describe and provide examples of how they perceived the methodology of PAAR and how they creatively applied it in various spaces they created. The process of the project is presented in the text as a move from inside out – from the creation of individual and personal PAAR spaces, through professional group spaces, and ended with setting up more public interdisciplinary PAAR spaces. While it was easy to open such spaces, the authors argue that the methodology represents a new relational culture that is difficult to sustain. The 'facilitation' performed by an individual or a team that can authentically and consistently maintain the values of PAAR is considered to be the 'tool' for achieving sustainability of PAAR.

The project

The goal of the Reflect-OR project in Bulgaria was to introduce and study the effect of PAAR in the field of career counseling. PAAR methodology focuses on the strengths of the practitioners, analyzes professional success and thus facilitates more conscious utilizations of the identified strengths and successful strategies in everyday professional practice.

Applying the methodology in Bulgaria was organized in three stages, chronologically planned in the project. The first stage was the training of three Bulgarian educators and researchers from the New Bulgarian University in PAAR theory and practice. The second stage required that the trainers facilitate 10 PAAR group sessions (laboratories) with career counselors. The third stage required further transfer of the PAAR methodology in other professional settings by the researchers and by the career counselors acquainted with the approach in the first two stages of the project. It involved the creation of special settings for the laboratories – both physical and relational which we, the project participants called 'PAAR spaces' – pockets of new culture. How was the PAAR space different from the Bulgarian cultural space? This was a key question.

PAAR stands for participatory and appreciative action and reflection. Each one of these four words suggests new and challenging processes in Bulgarian life. Participation of the people has become a theme of the public discourse after the democratic changes were supposed to start with the end of the totalitarian regime in 1989. The possibility to use the freedom to participate in the new democratic processes was hindered by the deeply set beliefs that the state was the major agent of change fostered during communist years. Additionally, Bulgaria suffered many centuries of Ottoman domination, which has left a stamp over the free participation of people in public spaces.

Regarding appreciation, there is a popular Bulgarian saying that has guided generations of parents: 'Modesty is what makes a person beautiful'. With this short sentence many people can associate their current difficulties to advance, to take a lead, to enjoy appreciation. Comparisons between members of a group rather than appreciation of one's capacities were used to foster the collective unity rather than the development of the individual. Again, the roots of this trait can be traced back to our history. It can be seen also as an effort to preserve the traditional patriarchal Bulgarian values that fitted to the value of equality and the collective fostered during socialism.

Action research and reflection are also new to the culture. First, research as an instrument to study reality was in conflict by the planned communist economy, which was difficult to study critically. Similarly, reflection on one's own practice was traditionally not encouraged as external criticism was the practice of evaluation of one's work achievements. In current times, as a country in transition, Bulgarians are bombarded by Western regulations, theories and methods, often in conflict with the traditional ones, which limits reflections and learning from experience. After the democratic changes started, reflective practice was firmly settled (mostly in the caring professions through supervision and the theories of individual development) as a tool for self-knowledge and exploration – the basis of PAAR.

The project that came before Reflect-OR was in the field of education. The first Reflect project focused on reflection on 'critical incidents' as turning points that would carry potential for learning and change in education. The goal of Reflect-OR was to transfer the results achieved during the first project but also to implement four 'turns' away from it. Those were from the deficit-based discourses 'towards the development of appreciative insight, understanding the root causes of success and sustaining strengths-based discourses'; from the self-to collective learning, from one way of knowing to an acceptance of more pluralistic view of ways of knowing, and from reflection to extract practical wisdom and act on its basis (Ghaye et al., 2008). Again, the goals of the new project – to introduce the 'turns' – were fenced by the traditional values of the culture. Studying success in Bulgaria sounds like a heresy among its citizens, who feel unhappier than the Haitians after the earthquake. Reflective practice even though known, is deficit-oriented (Bilson & Markova, 2007). In general, collective activities have been eroded both by the anomic processes in the society and as something that was overemphasized during communist years. Regarding the last two 'turns', addressing the pluralistic ways of knowing and the capacity to learn from practice and act upon this knowledge, Alexandrov (1998) states:

> All aspects of the education – rigid curricula, boring training techniques, preoccupation with discipline in the organization of the class work and outdoors activities, ritualized hierarchical interactions between teachers and students – are permeated by the understanding of learning as a one way process of instruction. The assumption about the social mission of education is that of molding on a mass scale the clay of the virgin minds in an appropriate form. The young are provided with the 'right' type of knowledge, indoctrinated in the 'correct' understanding of the world, coerced to adopt the 'true' version of reality, established once and forever and sanctioned by authority. Students are system-

atically discouraged to discover and experiment with innovative ideas, creativity is considered deviance, critical viewpoints are outlawed and often punished, and thinking is channeled in strictly set didactic models.

In summary, both the introduction of PAAR and the innovations it represented were challenges to the culture. The question was how.to facilitate PAAR that was based on autonomous participation and exploration in a culture that fosters dependency; how to encourage group collaboration in a culture which has corrupted the idea of the collective; how to contain positivity and appreciation in a deeply pessimistic society and how to study practice in an environment overwhelmed by foreign regulations. Finally there was the issue of how to introduce PAAR – another foreign methodology.

Below are presented the reflections of the project participants who experienced the two conflicting cultures in several PAAR spaces we opened. The first two examples are about the internal PAAR space we opened within ourselves as starting points of the change. The third one was about a group space that one of the career counselors created while teaching surfing. The fourth example is about how a community PAAR space was opened. What integrates these experiences of creating PAAR spaces in an anti-PAAR culture is discussed against the challenges stated above.

PAAR as an internal space (the story of the project coordinator)

As the coordinator of the Reflect-OR project in Bulgaria and as a person who felt new to both – the field of career counseling, and the PAAR methodology – what guided me at the beginning of my work was my training and practice in psycho-dynamic social work according to which opening any space in reality starts with opening the space within yourself. The more secure I would feel in and with this space, the more secure would be the project environment for experimenting with the new approach for learning through reflection. Luckily, the project in Bulgaria was flexible enough to allow me to start opening my own internal PAAR space before all other activities. Instead of following a pre-planned schedule with already selected groups of participants, it was possible to learn about the approach first and then start inviting career consultants to shape the group in Bulgaria.

The first PAAR setting was the administrative meeting of the project where the leaders of the project partners gathered together to discuss how to make the already set project frame consistent with the values PAAR – ensuring participation, appreciation of the contribution of the participants and their strengths, and reflection on the project's actions. The group comprised two career consultants – leaders in the field, the administration of the project – managers and researchers working in academia. Tony (the group's facilitator) was teaching us PAAR by facilitating the group in a way that everybody participated, that everybody's contribution was appreciated, that our activities were reflected upon and that we were learning from the process. We were planning our project, reflecting on the way we were planning it, while relating to each other appreciatively, learning from the process and guiding it further by planning the same experience in a way that more people feel it.

The physical space of the meeting was under the ground floor of a building. The space, created for educational purposes was comfortable and home-like. People who were at the meeting knew each other well: they had worked on the previous Reflect project or/and had previous training in PAAR. I was new to everybody and everybody was new to me. Nevertheless, I did not feel a stranger. My task for the meeting was to present the context of the career counseling in Bulgaria and I performed it. The team listened, questions followed and at the end suggestions were made how to plan the project in my country. There was a special space in the group that was created before I had become part of it. The pace was slow; there were moments of silence between the questions, the answers and the suggestions. I enjoyed the space. It allowed me to think about additional ideas, remember additional information, and reflect on my own presentation. I did not feel pressed to have answers to all questions. I was able to recognize my own uncertainties and doubts. I felt secure enough to disclose those. Feeling safe was the first building block of my internal PAAR space. This space facilitated my getting in touch with my own questions and thus made me open to learn.

The second key element of my internal PAAR space was the experience of freedom. Another task of the same meeting was to contextualize the pillars of PAAR by co-constructing their meaning in our multicultural team. ‘Participation’ was the PAAR pillar under discussion and the question our team struggled with was about what was the kind of participation we needed for our project. The group talked about how liberating but also how challenging and threatening participation can be. My thoughts got me back to the communist years when we, school girls and boys had to demonstrate how actively and enthusiastically we can march at the Labor Day on the May 1 during the obligatory parades. Thinking about the post-totalitarian context of Bulgaria, I shared that non-participation has been a form of active resistance against the totalitarian regime and therefore a very active form of participation. I added that even if the political situation has changed, this learned attitude is still alive even though it often blocks genuine participation in Bulgaria. The group did not comment but later the facilitator asked the group: ‘Shall we agree that our participation has to be active?’

I felt several things in that moment. First, I felt that my comment was heard and reflected upon. Second, I felt confronted with a rule that would not respect my own potential difficulties with participation. Third, I was confronted with a rule of the group. Fourth, I was given a choice to participate actively or to leave the project. Paradoxically, despite feeling conflicted, I experienced a wave of energy. This situation made me feel free. I chose to participate.

A couple of weeks later, I realized that in that moment I obtained a space to choose whether to participate or not. The question was why did I feel free? First, before I was confronted with the question, after I had already developed a feeling of safety in the group. Second, my explanation about the non-participation as a cultural type of participation was heard and it changed the definition of the term ‘participation’ that we planned to use in the project into the term ‘active participation’. My contribution changed the frame of the project. Third, the message that I received was ‘we know that you can actively participate but still it is your choice to do it or not’. I did not choose to participate because I did not have choice to refuse participating. Facing the choice, I had a freedom to choose and I chose the space where I had the freedom to make choices.

Back then I was not conscious about these processes. After my return to Sofia, sharing about the meeting, a member of the Bulgarian team told me that I was changed: I radiated enthusiasm. In summary, feeling safe, freedom to make choices and active participation were the pillars of my internal PAAR space. Still, I have got the space in a foreign country. Parallel processes of experiencing the same happened in the project team. After the meeting, feeling more prepared I started inviting people from the field of career counseling to participate in the project. Interestingly enough, the participants who decided to participate were those, either knowing (and I hope) trusting our team or those referred by others they trusted. Feeling safe became a shared experience even before the project started. In my inviting people I did not make efforts to convince them – the people had the choice to participate. In terms of the last 'pillar', the group actively participated throughout the project.

Opening PAAR space in the consulting room (the story of a career counselor)

I grew up in Bulgaria and still live there. It is sad to confess but here many people relate to each other without recognizing their strengths. Too often the topics of conversations are about who feel worse than the other one. The same is the situation in the professional practice. Unfortunately, I also used this model until I felt it suffocating. In the books I read that this behavior does not lead to anything good. I tried to see the world in a more positive way. I did not have success all the time but I kept trying. Talking about strengths during the labs confirmed my conviction that this is the path to success, to personal and professional development even though at the beginning it was difficult to discuss strengths only.

I tried to present PAAR ideas to my friends and they opposed. I took this reaction as something natural having in mind the attitudes of contemporary Bulgarians. I decided that I have to present PAAR not just as a theory, but to apply its ideas first to myself. I accepted that the relationship with the other person is mirror-like: that the other person reflects my own reaction; that whatever I present will be reflected back to me. This method did not always work and I did not always get the reaction I expected. The changes happened slowly and I needed to be patient.

I tried to apply PAAR in my professional life too. I used the same mirror-like communication. As a career counselor I meet people with very negative attitudes that hinder their personal and professional development. One day, a 34-year-old unemployed man asked for a consultation. He was arrogant and mistrustful. In a situation like this, it was normal for me to respond in a similar aggressive way. Nevertheless, I decided to use the mirror-like communication. First I thought that it was him who asked for help – who took the first step – and I tried to make him comfortable by creating a space for myself where I would feel safe and protected. The man, being accustomed to traditionally rejecting behavior, got confused. He left but I felt that the first seed was planted. In two days the man returned. He behaved differently. He was not aggressive and he participated actively in our conversation. He shared that our first meeting was different experience for him. He also explained how his long unemployment the stress the rejections from the others made him feel useless, which in turn made him aggressive and affected his wish to develop. The reason he returned to me was my different behavior. We started talking about his professional experience. Our relationship helped him to pass the stage where he was overwhelmed by his past negative experiences and to start planning for the future. I asked questions that encouraged the development of his creativity and his strengths. After we ended our meeting, he felt more secure and self-confident. In applying the PAAR methodology I succeeded to help the man to regain his hope.

Opening PAAR space in a group (The big waves and PAAR…or how to use our strengths when a two-meter-high wave falls on us and fills our ears with sand: a story of a career counselor)

The labs made me experiment with PAAR in situations where there was no hierarchy, formalities or rules. What made me write was that in order to make changes we need many additional circumstances. And the best thing about PAAR is that we can create them.

If a huge wave hits you and throws you on the sand you start experiencing the strange feeling of helplessness coupled with the question: 'Shall I recover this time?' Whatever strengths and skills we have it is not probable that we use them at such moments and look respectable with seaweed and sand covering your body. So I decided to study the effect of PAAR in such circumstances. I asked myself whether I would find a connection between knowing our strengths and ways of using them well, and learning when the things are outside our comfort zone and limits of our control.

I met a group of surfers who could not learn to surf despite their efforts. They shared that they were scared, that the conditions were not good or that their equipment was inadequate. These people did not have experience, theory or trust in their instructors. After several conversations with them, they started surfing. Their comments included: 'I cannot believe, I thought I would not ever be able to learn'.

How did this change happen?:

(1) It is important to be a good role model.

This group saw in me a person who could surf. I realized how important it is to show to others that you can cope in such a way that the others believe: that they can do this too, that they want it. I realized that they needed somebody next to them while they were learning. In this role, it was important to challenge them. Every time I set new tasks, new goals. I did not set the time frame for their achievements, which freed a lot of resources to take care of myself and to learn the things that I needed to learn myself.

(2) It is important to care.

I definitely cared about whether they would succeed and did not let them waste their time in negative beliefs.

(3) It is important to make small steps.

I provided them with practical information in small portions. I told them funny facts about hydrodynamics etc. that they could use and try. I learned how important curiosity was in studying and how many ways there are to make one interested in the things he/she does if you know his/her strengths.

(4) It is important to encourage many tries and provide feedback on those.

After every piece of information I left them to experiment. I asked them about what they felt and experienced. I watched how the things went better and easier, and how they started learning from their own experience. We were in touch not only during the 'classes' and we encouraged each other to try new things. The success of one person led to more successes in the rest and our satisfaction was incredible.

(5) It is important to recognize individual qualities.

Each one of the participants was different. I could tell each one of them why I thought he/she would succeed delving into their 'motivation', 'former successes', 'high spirit', 'consistency', 'personal style' and 'the specific way they needed support'. Even though I was not a psychologist, they asked me whether I was one. This opened new professional themes and opportunities for business ideas. All of them had one goal but everybody reached it in his/her own way. After this PAAR experience these people liked the taste of the sand in their mouths, the bruises on their knees, the hits of the waves. All their negative beliefs disappeared, and they felt desires for stronger wind, bigger waves and higher jumps. This change attracted more new fans in the group.

Even though I am not sure whether I have made any contribution to these people overcoming their fears, as a conclusion I would write that when you hit the right moment, the right people, the right attitudes and the right communication, and when there is mutual respect, inspiration and practice, the things sooner or later happen in the best possible way. And if any of these elements are absent, you can open the bag with the tools, take out PAAR and something else and start creating...until you fill the deficits.

Opening PAAR space in the community (the story of a project researcher)

This is the account of my attempt to practice PAAR apart from the work of the Sofia Reflect-OR project laboratory, applying the approach to the task of community development in rural Bulgaria. Inspired by the idea of opening new reflective spaces we – the Bulgarian team of the project – committed ourselves to identifying and utilizing the opportunities for experimenting with the approach and testing its applicability to various local contexts.

The context: the LEADER approach to community development

The specific approach to rural development, known as LEADER, originally evolved in EU in the 1990s as an attempt to invigorate the local economy of depopulated rural regions, creating incentives for the young people to live and work there. The aim of the program was to encourage sustainable development according to local potential, and the elaboration of new strategies and their implementation through strong focus on cooperative partnerships and networks. The philosophy and practice of LEADER is explicitly participatory – 'Decentralized, integrated and bottom up approach to territorial development' – and strongly relies on the voluntary involvement of the local community.

The LEADER approach in Bulgaria was slightly modified to address the major problem faced by the countryside in the transition period: continuous depopulation due to underdevelopment and lack of employment opportunities. The project was targeted at the most impoverished rural municipalities, and the explicit objective was to foster self-employment and entrepreneurship in agriculture, tourism, forestry and services.

The major goal of the project was to build local capacity for proper utilization of the forthcoming EU funding for rural development. The assumption was that at the end of the project local expert knowledge would emerge that was owned by the communities and enabling them to successfully grasp and use various opportunities for sustainable development. For this purpose the establishment and training of local action groups (LAG) as grassroots organizations, responsible for drafting and implementing strategies for local development, was crucial. The project aims to strengthen the capacity of municipal authorities, local farmers, land and forest owners, small and medium enterprises, non-governmental organizations, extension service providers, professional associations and cooperatives so as to become leaders in sustainable rural development. The mechanism for achieving those objectives is the establishment of local action groups.

LAGs were registered as non-governmental organizations with representation of various local stakeholders: businesses, citizens groups, professional associations, etc. Guided by local coordinators, these groups were actively involved in the process of establishing the rules and procedures of the work, developing the strategies, deign and implementation of pilot projects.

The field experience

My role in the community development projects informed by the LEADER approach was twofold: to facilitate meetings with the local people and organize client-tailored trainings for the 'informal leaders' in the community on various issues related to rural development such as needs assessment, participatory planning, mobilizing local resources, fostering innovative projects and social entrepreneurship, building cooperative partnerships and networks, etc. The philosophy of involvement and empowerment, inherent to the LEADER approach, was quite compatible with the spirit of PAAR, so I decided to take a step further from the requirements of the project and engage the participants in reflective learning experiences, informed by PAAR.

I started by presenting the method for my colleagues, responsible for the training and the meetings in the villages. They were intrigued and inspired, but also anxious as to how the method would be accepted by the local people, who hardly had any experience with community development work, let alone with participatory approaches. These concerns indicated one of the key factors of resistance to PAAR and reflective practice in general: the lack of trust on the part of professional developers in the capacity of the common people to reflect upon their experience and learn from it. The tacit assumption was that reflective learning was a sophisticated intellectual matter, accessible only to properly educated people. This assumption was mobilized to sustain social distinctions and thus reinforce a culture of dependency and alienation between the 'ordinary' people and the professional elites. On a deeper level of analysis, it can be seen as a social defense against anxieties provoked by genuine involvement with marginalized and impoverished people: the 'losers' of the economic and social transition in Bulgaria. Indeed, the concerns of the professional moderators about the capacity of the community to accept such a paradigmatic shift were partly justified, as the following incident will illustrate.

One of the start-up meetings of the project took place in the community hall in a small village at the Greek border, where all families owned vineyards and are grew grapes, although some of them had other jobs. The households were quite poor and the money earned by selling the production formed a considerable share of their income. That year the harvest was very good, but the price offered by the wine producers was poor because of the collapse of the market of Bulgarian wines. The people, who had expected a decent earning for their hard labor through the year, had to sell the grapes at a much lower price than the previous year. Naturally, they came to the meeting angry and frustrated, and instead of reflecting on the possibilities for innovative projects provided by the Program for Rural Development, they indulged in vicious accusations and blaming. The government, the municipal council and the mayor were suspected in conspiracy with the big wine-producing companies against the interests of the farmers. I was also attacked as an agent of the hostile government in my capacity of representative of a program launched by the Ministry of Agriculture. The program and the opportunities it offered were devalued: 'These projects are for the rich folk, the same people get all the money; we the common people are always at the losing side'; the good intensions of the experts were questioned and ulterior motives were attributed to our work: 'Why don't you tell us what money are you earning from that program?'

We became painfully aware that empowering the people to develop their own agenda of the meeting we had actually opened a Pandora's box. Faced with such a hurricane of distrust and suspicion, in a moment of despair we were at the point of acknowledging our failure and leaving the meeting ashamed and defeated. Fortunately, I managed to withstand the pressure and reframe positively this outburst of anger as a legitimate protest against the difficult circumstances with which they had to cope. This intervention gave immediate effect: the group calmed down, the people stopped shouting all in one voice and started to listen to one another and to us. This was the first step in containing the anxiety of the group and shifting the emotional dynamics of the meeting to a more constructive discussion: we appreciated the right of the participants to be angry and they responded by appreciating our empathy. This made possible a different perspective to be voiced and listened to in the group. Still, the paranoid, black-and-white picture of the situation was far from extinct, only that now we were seen not as enemy but as potential ally against the 'bad guys out there'.

In the ensuing discussion I suggested the farmers to organize and withstand their collective interest by bargaining a decent price for their production. It turned out that they had tried to form a sort of local trade union, but this attempt for collective action had proved futile: some of the members, pursuing their short-term private interest, had decided to sell at lower prices and had thus failed the agreement. This betrayal was quite discouraging for the rest and had reinforced the distrust and the individualistic survival mentality. Once again, the group regressed to a blaming mode, looking for a scapegoat, but this time the 'bad guys' were not outside, but within the community. When the passion was exhausted, the anger gave way to depression. A feeling of despair and self-contempt took over the group: 'We are good for nothing; we are not trustworthy people; we know only how to survive on one's own'. At this point I intervened again with the comment that they as a group have an opportunity to reflect upon this experience of failure and learn some important lessons for the future. They can either chose to follow the self-defeating strategy of individual survival or make another more adequate attempt for collective action. This time the group was silent and thoughtful for some time, and then an elderly man suggested that they remain after the meeting to discuss this idea among themselves. Finally the critical incident was over and we were able to pursue with the original agenda of our meeting. These same people listened attentively to the presentation of the program, asked relevant questions, participated quite positively in the discussion and identified a number of areas for local development.

This episode illustrates the challenges encountered by PAAR practitioners in cultures dominated by negative patterns of blaming and shaming, and puts forward the issue of the limitations of the approach and the need for its contextualization.

Entering the PAAR spaces

The project started at a university. The project group comprised of members of a university departments, career counselors from JobTiger (a business organization) and three other members who were caring professionals working in different settings.

Career counselors who chose not to participate in the project were those who worked in the state sector. In the first case the coordinator invited the potential participants individually in a private space where the consultant could hear about PAAR and ask questions. The coordinator had to invite the state consultants by writing an official latter to a ministry, and the ministry responded on behalf of the organization refusing to participate. It looked then as if the invitation itself was a necessary PAAR space, a transition to the group PAAR space. It turned out that the coordinator's assumption that attracting people into a PAAR space starting from opening space within the person who invited them was an illusion. At the end of the project it became clear that all of the participants entered the project space because this space was recommended by a person with whom they had already had a trustful relationship. Cornwall (2002) explores issues of power and difference in relation to how spaces for participation are created in development. She writes that the space is shaped by the way people enter it, and claims that it is different to invite people from people expressing rights to participate. In Bulgaria, another specific layer to this process was that it mattered whether the person who invites you to engage with PAAR was trusted.

Security and the PAAR relational space (facilitation and attachment theory)

A basic postulate of attachment theory – one of the most prominent theories that considers the role of the attachment relationship on individual development – is that only when the individual feels secure enough he/she can start exploring reality. This reality can be the reality of the external world but it can also be the inner reality of his/her world of emotions and states (Bowlby, 1973). When the caregiver is available and attentive to the child's needs, the child's is able to focus on these realities rather than checking the whereabouts of the caregiver. This interrelation between the two parties is the process that transforms the parent into a secure base for the child from which it can explore the environment (Bowlby, 1973, p. 236). This interrelation builds the child's sense of self because sensitive and responsive parenting forms the child's internal working model of him/herself as a valued individual whose communications with others are important. In contrast, unresponsive or abusive parenting creates an internal working model for the child of him/herself as an inadequate and unworthy person. Bretherton and Munholland (1999) summarized that people who had unresponsive parenting tend to interpret other people's behavior in a negative way and to expect rejection. People who had sensitive parenting tend to expect acceptance and respect from others. The repetition of this behavior can become unconscious and difficult to alter (pp. 89–90). Bowlby argued that the Internal Working Models (IWMs) are open to new information and can change and there is enough evidence that this happens both in the early and in the adult years of life (Main, Kaplan, & Cassidy, 1985). The key is a new relationship with an attachment figure that can provide security which facilitates security that the shared emotions can be reflected upon, respected and understood (Fonagy, Steele, Moran, Steele, & Higgitt, 1993). This though can be performed by the attachment figure only if her/his own experiences have been understood and reflected upon by an adult mind. Otherwise insecurities of the parent are likely to be transmitted to the next generation.

Minkov (2002) defined our patriarchal culture as anxiety-prone, meaning that members of the society feel anxious in uncertain situations instead of curious of exploring them. In contrast, Western societies enjoy novel events and value differences. There are fewer rules and people are encouraged to discover their own truth. Minkov argues that the familial organization of the Bulgarian society leads to an external locus of control and, consequently, to the need for predictability in the environment and dependency upon an authority figure. He claims that the patriarchal culture in Bulgaria is maintained by parenting that fosters anxiety in children by rearing them in a forbidding manner, which later makes people feel anxious when confronted with the unknown (p. 248). According to attachment research, security can be fostered within a relationship with a trusted authority figure who provides a new relational model (Main, Kaplan, & Cassidy, 1985). What somehow resonates with the above is some thoughts of our project's group:

> What kept me in the project was the power of the external authority figure. The farther an expert is from the work and the relationships in our team, the easier people hear from him and trust him, try to experiment with their practice' and 'only facilitation from a foreign culture can foster change in the group.

The above suggests that PAAR is welcomed because individuals are wired to seek security in relationships within which they would be appreciated, their needs met and their achievements acknowledged and reflected back. The question is how to sustain the feeling of security that PAAR brings in the culture. It is important to note here that the matter of sustainability is not just a question that relates to the project's goals. It is a question that has direct link to the ethics of opening PAAR spaces because according to attachment theory, changing 'parenting' styles is disruptive to development of individuals because again, the feeling of security is minimized. In summary, in relation to the Bulgarian culture, the PAAR space of fostering active participation, different ways of collective learning, appreciation of success is new to the Bulgarian culture and its sustainability depends on a lasting and secure PAAR relationship. Below is what a project member shared:

> At the beginning of the project I was not clear to what extent the Bulgarian project team were engaged with the project. I had a feeling that the things would dissolve after the project ended and that it would not be possible to continue working on the project together. At the beginning there was no communication between the leaders of the Bulgarian (BG) team and there was a feeling that I was serving somebody else's interests rather than participating for myself. With the time this changed.

How did this change happen? The following summarizes the group's thinking: 'What made me keep participating in the labs was the field of interest, the nice space in the group and of course the facilitator'. To make the PAAR space sustainable in the Bulgarian context, it needed to be modeled. Before entering the role of PAAR facilitators, it was important for all members of our teams to experience the PAAR facilitation with its author (Tony) for a longer time than planned for the project. He committed to the task by planning two additional visits for the Bulgarian laboratories.

Last weekend two of the 'graduates' of the project started their first PAAR group. As the reader can imagine, most of the nine members of the group are people who did not have trustful relationships with the leaders. Still, they have become members of the group to learn how to become facilitators. They were not invited: they expressed their right to participate. The PAAR space is changing (see Figure 1).

Conclusions

In the Bulgarian part of the Reflect-OR project, opening space for PAAR started with invitation from a person whom the future participants trusted. After participating in 10 labs facilitated by the author of PAAR, some of the participants applied the approach either in their professional field, or in informal spaces as the stories above present.

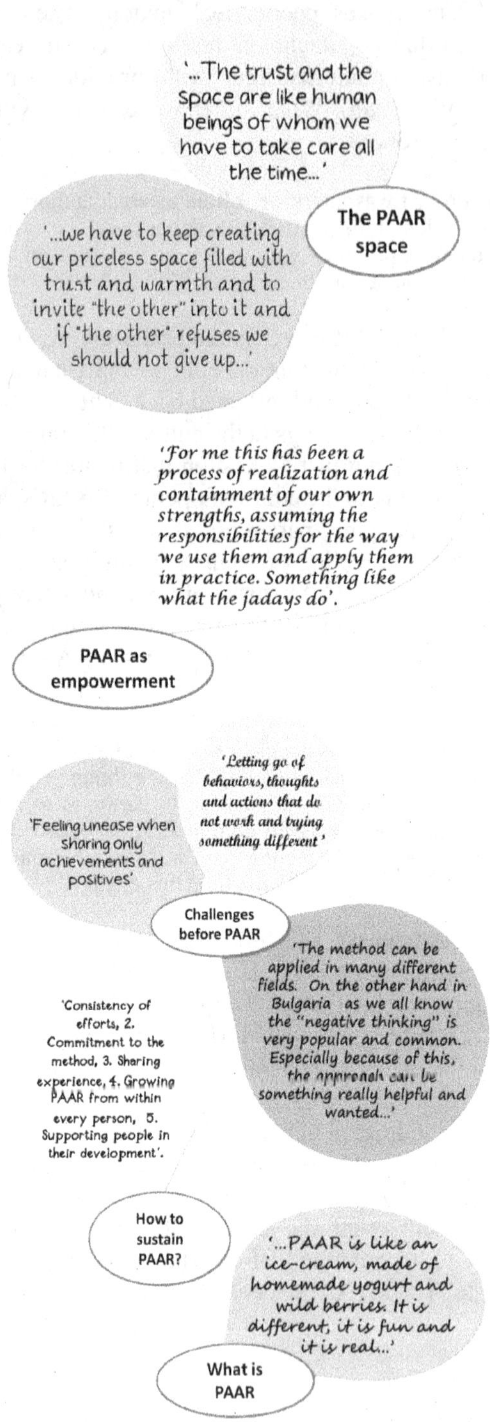

Figure 1. PAAR-in-practice.

What appears especially difficult here is to behave PAAR-like in the grim institutional cultures that most Bulgarians abide. The values implicit in this approach are so often at odds with the basic assumptions underlying those cultures that engaging genuinely with PAAR might easily put the individual in tension, if not in conflict, with the organizational mainstream. In effect, people who enthusiastically engage with PAAR in the protected space of a group event are likely to relapse to the alienated and pessimistic mode of social participation in their daily work contexts.

The major conclusion is therefore the need for contextualizing PAAR in the specific environment in order to give it a chance to get integrated in the culture of the respective community or institution. This entails not only careful gearing of the approach to the capacity of individual participants to accept and embrace changes in their perspective, but also to the capacity of the culture to integrate and sustain those changes without threatening its equilibrium. This means establishing lasting relations with people in organizational roles who are open to PAAR and developing those relations in time, respecting the organizational idiosyncrasy and responding positively and supportively to its often modest propensity to learn and change. Such humble and culturally sensitive strategy can trigger, we believe, profound transformation of both individual mindsets and cultural patterns.

References

Alexandrov, H. (1998). Social participation in post-totalitarian society. *Annual of Bourgas Free University,* Vol. 1. Bourgas: Bourgas Free University.

Alexandrov, H., & Kabakcieva, P. (2008). Development of rural regions: A comparative study. In *Sociological Review.* Sofia: Sofia University.

Bilson, A., & Markova, G. (2007). But you should see their families: Preventing child abandonment and promoting social inclusion in countries in transition. *Social Work and Social Sciences Review, 12*(3), 57–78

Bowlby, J. (1973). *Attachment and loss: Vol. 2. Separation.* New York: Basic Books.

Bretherton, I., & Munholland, K. (1999). Internal working models in attachment relationships. In J. Cassidy & P. Shaver (Eds.), *Handbook of attachment: Theory, research, and clinical applications* (pp. 89–115). New York: Guilford Press.

Cornwall, A. (2002). *Making spaces, changing places: Situating participation in development.* Brighton: Institute of Development Studies.

Fonagy, P., Steele, M., Moran, G., Steele, H., & Higgitt, A. (1993). Measuring the ghost in the nursery: An empirical study of the relation between parents' mental representations of childhood experiences and their infants' security of attachment. *Journal of American Psychoanalytic Association, 41*, 957–989.

Ghaye, T., Melander-Wikman, A., Kisare, M., Chambers, P., Bergmark, U., Kostenius, C., and Lillyman, S. (2008). Participatory and appreciative action and reflection (PAAR) – Democratizing reflective practices. *Reflective Practice, 9*(4), 361–397.

Main, M., Kaplan, N., & Cassidy, J. (1985). Security in infancy, childhood and adulthood: A move to the level of representation. In I. Bretherton & E. Waters (Eds.), *Growing points in attachment theory and research* (pp. 66–104). *Monographs of the Society for Research in Child Development*, 50, Serial No. 209.

Minkov, M. (2002). Why are we different. Multicultural differences in family, society, and business. Sofia, Bulgaria: Classic and Style.

Login and logout: practices of resistance and presence in virtual environments as a kind of reflective learning activity

Simona Marchi[a] and Emma Ciceri[b]

[a]*Department of Economics, 'Sapienza' University of Rome, Rome, Italy and Reflective Learning Italy, Rome, Italy;* [b]*Trade Marketing and Innovation, Postal S.p.A., Rome, Italy*

Learning processes are closely connected to the contexts in which professional and day-to-day practices are conducted, and to the characteristics of those contexts. These processes develop through and between different systems of activities, established by actors operating on the basis of explicit and implicit rules in order to achieve certain goals. They do so through the use of artefacts and knowledge, within a system of labour sharing, role definition and specific power mechanisms.

What happens when the rules of these systems, or the roles, artefacts or knowledge, change? What happens to learning processes if the contexts in which the practices are implemented happen to be online, for example in a blog or a virtual community of practice (VCoP) or on social networking platforms? When we speak of learning in Web 2.0 environments created *ex novo* within a project, we are speaking of a type of participation and precise presence that does not manifest itself through a nomadic, solitary journey around the web. It is, rather, considered as one of the ways of being, learning and working together within a given project. This is, therefore, a very powerful option: learning together online through the use of ICT and in a given space of time.

Our intention in this paper is to develop a two-fold reflection on learning modes in virtual activity systems: the importance of learning as participating (learning to participate); the importance of learning to learn together in virtual environments (learning together). In so doing, we refer to the experience of using web instruments in the context of a European project in which guidance practitioners from a number of different countries took part. Lastly, the general lines of a participatory and appreciative approach to facilitating online reflective learning will be proposed.

Introduction

The learning processes that take place through web environments developed *ex novo* and for a set, albeit on average long, period of time (e.g., one year), involve learning:

(1) together with others who sometimes know one another, at other times do not;
(2) synchronously or asynchronously;
(3) the mechanisms of presence/absence and online participation; and
(4) with and through the use of technology.

The aspects that need to be taken into consideration before embarking on a reflection on learning methods in relation to virtual activity systems are essentially two:

- Learning together: learning the methods of interaction and exchange through the relationship between technology and participants. How does technology activate individual and collective modes of online interaction and, vice versa, how does the way in which we use web resources transform our sense of the technology involved? How does learning develop through these interactions?
- Learning to participate: learning the sense and methods of online participation. What are the mechanisms of online participation: the drivers, resistance, duration, continuity (or lack of it) of online presence, the relationship between on- and offline? What does online participation mean?

This paper will seek to respond to the questions asked above and propose a way to facilitate online participatory and appreciative reflective learning.

Learning together through virtual environments

The first aspect, 'learning together', creates a relationship between practitioner community and virtual environment. According to Wenger, White, and Smith (2009), a community of practice that acts in virtual activity systems can be defined as a community of practice if learning is its central characteristic and fundamental goal. The distinguishing feature of such communities is, therefore, a sharing of the practices of presence, writing, publication and online production for the purpose of personal and professional improvement for individuals and communities, through specific learning processes. We are speaking, therefore, about online practices whose main objective is learning through participation and the sharing of ideas, experiences and emotions, and not the production of a given output envisaged by an organisation.

It is necessary, therefore, to distinguish between team and community of practice. Taking the definition of community of practice chosen here, the team cannot be considered as such a community since the central element linking the members of a team is not learning in itself, but reaching a given organisational goal and/or solving a given problem through rules, timescales and roles established in a given organisation. This does not mean that there is no learning involved in this process, but learning is not its main aspect.

In communities of practice, learning becomes the central element. Participants become learning partners and depart temporarily from the formal roles established by their organisations. In this respect, 'learning together depends on the quality of relationships, of trust and mutual engagement that members develop with each other' (Wenger, White, & Smith, 2009, p. 8). This distinction is important because it enables us to focus on learning as the goal of online practices and helps us understand why many virtual communities of practice (VCoP) initially established as online extensions of work teams operating in given organisations have not achieved the desired results.

By virtual environments we mean here online contexts co-generated through the joint use of different platforms and applications, and characterised by learning together. These environments may be placed on an institutional footing with clearly defined boundaries, like VCoPs (virtual communities of practice), or they may be distributed over networks and take shape through the joint use of a number of different resources. In the experience we acquired during the European project we sought to link the two types and tried to establish an environment that could take on the features of a VCoP but at the same time retain a vision of technology understood as social practice (Suchman, Blomberg, Orr, & Trigg, 1999). This is based on the co-definition and simultaneous co-design of the virtual environments and of the community of practice that was being established. The idea guiding us was that the development of a system 'is not the creation of discrete, intrinsically meaningful objects, but the cultural production of new forms of material practice' (Suchman et al., 1999, p. 394).

On the basis of a review of the literature on VCoPs and a study of at least 18 VCoPs, Dubé, Bourhis, and Jacob (2003) have constructed a typology that considers 21 structural characteristics organised into four main dimensions: demographic, organisational context, membership features and technological environment. Within each dimension, each of the 21 characteristics may vary along a continuum defined by two poles. This means that as these 21 structural characteristics vary we will in turn obtain a variety of VCoPs. This study shows that what holds an online CoP (community of practice) together is not so much the choice of technological instruments, i.e. the way in which the virtual environment (VE) in itself is structured, but the new idea of social relations that the interaction between the CoP and the VE manages to co-generate and support.

Considering the relationship between technology, community and learning therefore means placing the emphasis on the term 'practice'. This is a strong epistemological option that many authors have already addressed in the field of practice-based study. Most notably, in her article *From community of practices to practices of a community: Brief history of a travelling concept*, Gherardi (2008) underscores that forms of on- and offline collaboration have put the very idea of CoP (community of practice) to the test. She suggests that a transition be made from the concept of community of practices to that of practices of a community (PoC), where reflection remains connected to practice and so to forms of coordination and interaction.

The characteristics of practices and their sociological interest lies not so much in their variability but in their repetition, in their recursivity (Gherardi & Bruni, 2007), in their function of social reproduction and the construction of identity. In this recursivity, artistic talent, creativity and the capacity and intent to innovate, change and invent are developed. In studying online learning practices, we need to develop the variability and creativity associated with practices that manifest themselves as elementary and repetitive, i.e. technically directed to reproducing the place/context. Web 2.0 environments, in truth, change constantly in their content, the outcome of their expressive forms and their effect on participants, even though they are built and maintained through practices 'reproducing' the resources themselves.

Learning to participate in virtual environments

The second aspect, 'learning to participate', focuses on learning as participation and, at the same time, on participation as the outcome of a learning process. Sfard (1998) suggests two metaphors for learning: the acquisition metaphor and the participation metaphor.

The first metaphor for learning refers primarily to an accumulation (having) of information (knowledge), the aim of which is individual enrichment through the acquisition and possession of concepts and processes. Knowledge is understood as something that exists independently of actors. It can be acquired, possessed and organised by concept, material, content, notions, models and facts.

The second, the participation metaphor, sees learning as a goal linked to doing together that begins with an individual's learning to become an active participant, an activity that enables the group to be set up and produce knowledge (knowing) and learning through a process of reflection on individual and collective experience.

The metaphor for learning as a participation process is particularly well suited to virtual environments configured through social software applications that have been developed to support interaction within a group (Shirky, 2003) in which both learning and the production of knowledge are situated within relationships and distributed networks. At the same time, the metaphor for learning as an acquisition process is useful because it highlights another form of learning – and so of participation in communities – that is based on a different system of expectations. Participants in this learning process may be motivated by one or the other approach, or by both.

The decision to engage in social interaction, dialogue and exchange in virtual environments, especially by those who are driven by the logic of participation, depends on the existence of certain key elements. These include, first and foremost:

(1) considering interaction and the sharing of experience as a value;
(2) knowing and respecting the ethical implications of online interaction; and
(3) developing a reflective learning process based on valorising the individual and collective experiences of the group of participants.

For those attracted to the logic of acquisition, 'frequenting' virtual environments depends on:

(1) well-organised documents and content;
(2) ease of access and use; and
(3) constant up-dating of archives and the way they are structured.

A necessary condition for participation/fruition is, in any case, the creation of an environment (Schön, 1983). This step could seem forced with respect to the freedom offered by Web 2.0 as regards opportunities, including random ones, for sharing, creating and learning. However, an individual's choice to engage personally and learn by developing connections and ways of collaborating and by producing and sharing knowledge online means that modes of interaction and exchange that have certain characteristics must be defined.

The participatory dimension of online learning together (Jacobs, 2006) means not just individual participation but also creating the conditions for greater inclusion of different ways of knowing, understanding and seeing our own and other people's experiences. This means considering differences as a useful learning resource, but also recognising the value and validity of different voices through a shared process of participatory and deliberative democracy amongst equals (Phillips, 1995).

To be secure, virtual environments do not necessarily have to be private, closed and protected from outside eyes. It is the quality of the interaction and relationships created there that makes an environment secure. An environment perceived by participants as secure is in general characterised by interactions that are intended to appreciate, value and systematise, often creatively, the positive aspects and strong points of individual and collective contributions. In other words, an environment that produces value and/or objects of value, understood as:

> terms, gestures, behaviours, objects, that give the impression that what happens or circulates does indeed have a density, objectivity or a solidity that compels the modification of attitudes, the undoing of presuppositions and changes of opinions, or the reversal of precedent. (Latour, 2007, p. 227)

The value produced within an environment conceived for online learning does not lie solely in the production of knowledge but also in its distribution, sharing and co-generation. Reciprocity, a key aspect of online interaction practices, is expressed in terms of objects, emotions and content that are shared and exchanged on the basis of recognising the other within a relationship of trust based on listening, receptiveness, and valorising individual contributions.

The different types of valorisation are a function of participation, individual and group objectives, and the forms taken by interaction practices and by individual expectations and reputational dynamics, and *vice versa*. All these elements are in turn influenced by the valorisation modes that are generated and eventually become established within the group. Processes of constructing positive online reputational aspects are underpinned by appreciative ways of valorising the contributions offered by different participants. These refer to the group's ability to grasp and valorise the positive potential of individual or group experiences.

Login and log-out. Resistance, presence, participation and learning in virtual environments

The importance of the two levels; fruition and communication

> I found the VCoP very interesting for document consultation. I opened the things I found there, in effect it seemed very useful because it allows you to share files and material. As a communication system I personally have some difficulties, I mean I don't like using these tools. I normally use the network email service – very trite, I realise.
>
> It's only for the immediacy factor, rather than entering a site or a forum, something that means, on a day-to-day basis, when you've got a lot to do, a step that is pretty trivial in itself, but which doesn't come easily to me...to be frank.... And then I find that the communicative aspect always needs to be connected to a human, face-to-face process. It needs to be linked to a job that you do in person, with a considerable degree of continuity and intensity, otherwise the remote communication channel, by itself, risks being a space that in my opinion tends to wither away. For me it's more convenient, therefore, to consider the levels: use of the material, sharing of the 'to-do-list', internal communication system, communication with the outside world: who we are and what we're doing. (COL practitioner)

The viewpoints of the users taking part in virtual communities can be considered at a double level (see Figure 1):

(1) the level of choice (external or internal driver); and
(2) the motivation level (personal level of involvement, the motivational dynamics leading to the participant deciding to be there, to listen, give, receive, as well as the meaning that the act of presence assumes for those performing it).

These are substantive levels. As Turkle (1995) asserts, the apparent intrinsic structural weakness of virtual communities, contrasted with the strong structure of real societies, in actual fact makes it possible to establish community-based constraints on the basis not of power relationships but of free choices based on an affinity of interests. From this perspective, such weaknesses are transformed into a positive value.

We can imagine four macro-areas of reference that are generated by the intersection of the two levels. These help us to identify the main types of participation by seeking to answer two fundamental questions. The first: What leads individuals to take part in virtual communities? And the second: How can we organise these communities in such a way as to facilitate and strengthen active and virtuous participation?

We should first consider the choice axis. In this case, there may be a response to a request or to an external stimulus, of an institutional nature (with a limited involvement by the user, which leads to a possible temporary relationship). Examples might be the participation of a group of managers selected from the company's senior management to find a solution to specific market needs, or a team representing the different realities taking part in a project. Or there may be an informed personal choice (with a strong motivation and high degree of commitment, guarantees of a lasting relationship) based on the ethics of the relationship. Here, an example might be a group of volunteers organising network support activities for people in difficulty.

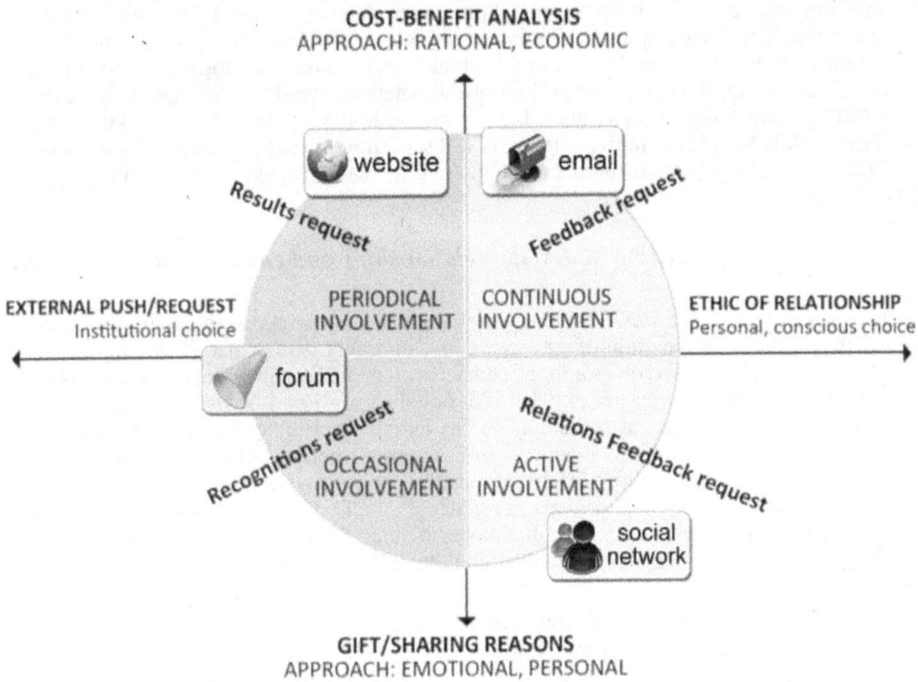

Figure 1. Axes of choice and motivation.

This axis intersects with the motivation axis. Here the response may be rational and economical, based on a cost-benefit analysis of the individual's participation in a project, activity or group. Or it may be emotional and based on attention to others, to people, colleagues and relationships, and inspired by the concept of the gift.

Each choice and each approach entails a different 'being there' in virtual relationships, as well as different expectations.

To date, many virtual communities are considered at the theoretical level as static and vertical structures (e.g., bottom-up: access, motivation, online socialisation, information giving and receiving, knowledge construction, development). These take into account roles and elements that can intersect perfectly (e.g., technology, learning, moderating). This type of schematisation (Berge & Collins, 1996) does not, perhaps, respond in full to the 'emotional' and motivational dynamics that are typical of online experience.

Web 2.0 social networks are polymorphous and in constant flux. Micro-groups and communities therefore manage and develop processes that can often be unexpected, on different levels that do not always coincide with pre-structured models.

The importance of the group and of synchronous interactions

> I was reflecting on this because I've not visited the site yet. I've had some experience of other, similar sites and suchlike and it's always been the case that, after the first five days, we don't know what to say to each other. Because the thing I find interesting, in effect, is the group dimension, and if we can't all be there together at the same time in a virtual environment, that's what makes the difference, as I see it. We either need to arrange a

> date and time, or else it becomes something much more operational. But that's not the interesting part, in my opinion. The interesting part is the reflection you can engage in together when you stop and say: 'Let's all think about this question together'. Otherwise, there's a time-lapse between when I write and when somebody replies, and that creates a distance and a slip in the relationship. In the meantime, I'll have been thinking other things, while the person replying to me is still referring to what I wrote a while ago, and I might even have written another piece in the intervening period. (COL practitioner)

The desirability of learning to develop relationships and communication remotely

> It seems to me that the way we feel is very common. I interpret this in two ways. On the one hand, the predisposition of age, as we are, in reality, somewhat grown up. On the other hand, our work involves a lot of contact with people, so it's our job to have direct relationships with service users. That's definitely true. But it's also true that this is maybe an occasion that in some way forces us into a privileged situation: we're not speaking about a forum of strangers but of a situation where we know each other, so for us it would be an opportunity for discussion and debate. Just as we tell our 50-year-old users that not knowing how to use a computer is simply out of the question, I'm afraid that we need to say the exact same thing to each other: the further on we go, the more of these virtual meeting opportunities there will be. (COL practitioner)

In a virtual community, working contexts should follow an approach based on transparency and consistency. Complex communities are often not located in a single virtual 'place', but are spread over several locations, each of which will have its own precise functions, typicality (and technical specifications), limits and potential. It is important, therefore, to ensure that each location clearly has and is clearly characterised by these features, so that users know what to expect when they enter.

Spaces and environments should not be considered as unique or unequivocal: the example of the Reflect-OR VCoP experience demonstrated that every so often a multiplication of spaces over time, to the disadvantage, perhaps, of the amount of content, makes it possible to set dynamics in motion that would otherwise be inhibited.

A 'network presence' in so many locations on the web (email, Facebook pages, dedicated social networks, project intranets, LinkedIn and others) should be analysed as a whole so that the dynamics set in motion between the members of the group can in turn be better analysed, and from a wider perspective: a perspective that takes into account not just the initial goals (or which does not stop at simple reporting of successes or failures in achieving objectives) but also the road embarked upon by individuals and the micro- and macro-groups that often do not follow a single, clear-cut path and which often contain an element of the unexpected.

This makes it necessary to continuously follow the evolution of this path and to highlight the positive and fruitful elements on a case-by-case basis. It is also necessary, of course, to seek to understand the reasons for any absences, problems or intricacies and to find, together with the group, the best solutions to prevent any gaps or critical situations arising.

The experience of the Reflect-OR VCoP project is an obvious example of how important it is to transform, when necessary, the locations and ways of meeting online.

This community of practice, linked to the European project of the same name, was created with the primary intention of connecting, on a number of levels, participants in the different countries involved (Italy, UK, Bulgaria and Switzerland). It was therefore, and necessarily, conceived as a simple and fairly traditional place: an intranet that enables dialogue with the www.ref-or.eu website and exchange of files of all types (images, text, audio-visuals, etc.). Also envisaged was the possibility of making relevant files visible in the public area of the site too.

Over the first two months we very soon realised that it was not sufficient to meet the needs of the project team. Indeed, the team was looking for other ways (in addition to face-to-face meetings and emails) to involve task force members and, above all, to engage in dialogue with participants in the different European countries involved. The first change en route was, therefore, the addition of an internal instant messaging area. This was followed by a limited-access forum that was fairly successful, albeit for a relatively short period. The next step, with the project already under way, was to create a dedicated social network. In this case, arrangements for participation were less controlled and guided, and as a result more free and less closely tied to the project context. At the same time, however, the communication made possible by the forum helped to consolidate interpersonal relations in a different way, through a more emotional and direct approach and on issues that were broader in scope.

Taken together, these places and types of interaction make up a very complex and dynamic universe, with dark corners and bright spots, linked both to the time factor and to the chain – whether or not one is actually achieved – of feedback from other users. It was extremely interesting to note, in the periods immediately following face-to-face meetings, that there was a peak in access and a greater amount of input to the various virtual locations. On the social network, more numerous in the case of internal meetings between project team and individual task forces, and in the institutional area, more numerous when the meetings involved the teams at the international level.

Overcoming performance anxiety and starting from the shared experience

> The VCoP is the virtual space of a group that has shared an experience: an experience that started in the Reflect project and concerned the reflective approach and our profession, but which then expanded to other contexts, because it spread to other contexts. So there isn't, or shouldn't be, any performance anxiety: 'Oh my God, what should I say? Does it make sense? Is it OK or not?' If we think of a particular piece of content as being linked to the VCoP or to this group, that means that we thought it might be something that should be shared with the others, with this group…. (COL practitioner)

Let the fact of thinking of a group of project partners select the content

> I thought that the fact of thinking about this group in some way selects the type of subjects dealt with. It wouldn't occur to me to talk to them about a volleyball game, a subject that has never even come up in our reflections. So maybe the distinguishing factor is in itself inherent to the type of group we are. And nothing prevents anyone from saying 'I'll give you a song', but at that point the thing you're touching, experiencing, isn't the content but the feelings you've been receptive to. (COL practitioner)

Participation, the difficulty of recognising yourself in what you write and the freedom to leave a reflection

> Normally, when I write something and then read it back I find it really hard to recognise myself in what I've written. So I thought of this as a gift: I write something and leave that reflection there for the group. If I have to think of using the VCoP, then I can think of using it to leave a reflection. If I give you a gift, it's because it gives me pleasure to

> do so. If I start thinking along the lines of 'I gave you a little present yesterday, what are you going to give me today?' then there's a very high risk that I'll feel constrained or that there'll be a lack of giving-and-taking of gifts. (COL practitioner)

Pathways of choice (choosing whether and how to be present) are key elements both to understand expectations and to suggest medium-term goals, even once the project has ended. Participants in turn established little transverse groups and stayed in touch using different tools and in different locations on the web, for example Facebook. The network in reality is not just a virtual mirror of real places, but a place-means, which you can cross, live in, own, explore or govern. An apt metaphor is parkour, an urban activity (or discipline) defined in France as *art du déplacement,* the art of displacement. Participants have to overcome any type of obstacle on their route by adapting their bodies to the surrounding environment.

So sharing and 'taking ownership of' spaces is both the goal and the means of being present on the web. A primary task of facilitators (who may be 'parkour instructors', or teach participants how to give their best possible performances within a space without 'getting hurt') is to 'prepare and prepare themselves for change', while preserving the clarity of intent and transparency of the relationships within the group and between participants.

Reciprocity as a way of valorising other people's contributions and stabilising affective-emotional dynamics

> One thing comes to mind: it's true that if I give someone a gift, I don't need to address the problem of getting something in exchange. It's also true, however, that we're maybe not all that aware of the emotional impact of the significance of these exchanges to the relationship, even if they're made in a virtual space.
>
> It's true that if I start an internal process in which I invest at the emotional level and don't get any in return from it, then I view that as a negative experience. I put myself in the shoes of somebody who has offered some content of value that has some form of relational value and doesn't get anything back.... It's true that we shouldn't expect something in return at all costs, but what comes back to me at an emotional level is a sense...everyone can have their say.... Maybe it would be useful to reflect and be aware: recognise the value of what the others are contributing and valuing it.
>
> If someone is brave enough to break through a wall of silence that is physical and has emotional depth, maybe there should also be an awareness on our part. We should recognise that and make an effort in that direction. We should give it value, which can also take the form of saying: 'I don't know what to say to you but I'm thinking of you'. Send a message, anyway, that you're there for that person. (COL practitioner)

Accountability, support and respect for people giving something of themselves in the network

> In the day-to-day dynamics of our work, with the huge amounts of emails we get all the time and that we often don't read, or just skim through, there's a risk that the episodic fragmentation of the relationship could generate a feeling that we're not accountable. So there's a lack of cohesion and of recognition, and of a sense of responsibility towards others. It's like in a Mastandrea film, where the singer throws himself off the stage and

> the audience opens up and he crashes to the ground. At the end of the day it's an act of faith, letting yourself go completely, letting something of yourself go. It's something that's played out over several levels, even a request for help or for someone to listen. (COL practitioner)

Online practices as reflective learning activities

On the basis of what we have said so far, we can state that online learning practices are also reflective learning practices if they:

- are conceived as a set of specifically situated social practices that are conducted in relation to individual and collective objectives that from one situation to the next are redefined and hinge upon learning processes;
- foster reflection on participants' own experiences and those of the other participants, as well as synchronous and asynchronous reflection during the online practice itself with respect to participants' own way of inhabiting a virtual environment and helping to generate value and learning;
- are based on forces of inclusion and, at the same time, of distinction/valorisation amongst participating practitioners. These are in part institutional in nature, defined in relation to the characteristics of the virtual environment and the roles identified in it; and in part negotiated through interactions and a redefinition of the modes of presence/participation;
- enable the emergence and activation of a virtual reality produced socially, and therefore in conditions of flux, in which participants are immersed and in which they participate by co-determining that reality;
- make it possible to establish a relationship that is both epistemic and pragmatic with day-to-day practices internal and/or external to the community;
- activate and stabilise participatory democratic processes;
- enable individuals and groups to express and reorganise their knowledge, opinions and purposes in an appreciative manner; and
- have a retroactive effect on the practices themselves and on the modes of participation.

The difficulties are many:

- Exclusion mechanisms can be very powerful and may act in a non-uniform manner.
- Virtual environments are subject to constant reformulations that always involve temporary stabilisation stages.
- The rapid obsolescence of knowledge and experiences in the network makes it difficult to identify ways of valorising participation and the contribution brought by each participant.
- The often asynchronous modes of connection mean that it is crucial to choose the content to be shared and the way to share it, given the different ways in which participants use that content.
- The reputational aspects are of great importance and regulate participants' choices in terms of practices, identity and connection styles. These aspects are variable and can generate tensions, all the more so when relationships include heterogeneous actors and purposes.

- Misalignments or 'anti-programmes' are always present in each online learning practice and may undermine relationships or encourage a frequent reformulation of common goals and values.
- The marked variability in practices in the use of Web 2.0 resources, since decisions, practices and knowledge affect multiple fields of action.
- The tension between appreciative modes designed to value individual contributions and silence/absence is the narrow line on which new forms of online power are played out. These can increase the rhythm of practices in virtual environments at a dizzying rate or else discourage participation.
- Participants' expectations as to modes of participation and presence online of the other vary according to the type of content (affective-emotional, professional, institutional, friendship-based, cultural, etc.) and the urgency of the response.
- The overall effect of online practices may not satisfy the expectations of individual participants, who may decide to abandon the community.
- Some issues could occupy most of the spaces for discourse and this could diminish the sense of 'citizenship' felt by those who feel for some reason that they are excluded from these issues. This can undermine democratic participation. When this happens, any increased rigidity on the part of the coordinators/facilitators in defining rules for participation may cause some participants to leave.

Facilitating appreciative and reflective learning in virtual environments

Virtual environments can also be and are, in fact, environments in which learning simply 'happens' (Amin & Roberts, 2006). However, in this paper we are referring to online practices whose aim is to share knowledge, experiences and emotions in order to foster the development of learning processes by individuals and/or a group.

This may seem to force the issue with respect to the high level of serendipity associated with online journeys experienced at various times of the day by users spread across different countries. The qualities, however, that encourage participation in virtual environments, and self-selection by participants, are the clarity of the objectives and the way in which the interactions take place. Taken together, these elements – the central role of learning, clarity of objectives and modes of interaction –sometimes require the presence of one or more facilitators. Facilitation is conducted through different roles and forms of communication, depending on the online environment in which it is developed. This type of support, whether online or offline, is provided at both the intellectual and the emotional levels.

Wenger, White, and Smith (2009) identify a form of leadership emerging from the relationship between new technologies and communities, which they call 'technology stewardship'. This has the task of helping communities to construct and live in digital habitats, operating both at the level of technological choices and through support for their use within the practices of a community. This is a form of valorisation both of what happens spontaneously in the community and of what happens on the basis of a given plan and/or schedule. This is often a competence distributed throughout the community rather than focused in any one individual.

If we consider both the specific characteristics of a facilitator and the new form of leadership mentioned above, it is possible to configure a new form of online facilitation defined as appreciative stewardship. This flanks the concept of technology stewardship with that of leader as steward (Senge, 1998); that is, a leader who is able to facilitate the construction of a collective vision, starting by valorising different viewpoints and listening to individual stories.

The concept of appreciative stewardship is not new. It came into being as a term concerning servitude and was linked to the responsibility and ability to 'take care of' everything that a house and the lives within it encompass. Various spheres have been used and in some way transformed the concept of steward.

Undoubtedly, the religious world is still today the one in which 'stewardship', and 'appreciative stewardship' in particular, is most widely used. We need only think of the custom of donations, the work of care, the responsibility for the development of a community, the ability to activate the donor community with respect to a shared vision of the development of the religious community. But it applies also and above all to the ability to say 'thank you', to recognise each other, and the significance of the other, and to make all participants (donors) feel that they are integral to the development of the community.

This concept is also used in the spheres of education and healthcare. In the former case it refers primarily to teaching and human resource organisation. In the latter, it refers mainly to treating the ill and the specificities of the relationship with the person being cared for. The central aspect is its origin, linked to: 'taking care of'; the development of an organisation, of a community and its members; mutual responsibility in collective development; the recognition of the other as a subject who brings value (in various forms) and who contributes, since that subject is also responsible; as well as the development of a community.

It is above all with reference to this last stage that it is possible to consider the concept of 'appreciative stewardship', understood as a form of distributed, online leadership based on the positive valorisation of participants' different perspectives and viewpoints and on a recognition of the value brought by each to the learning processes within the community. This concept is important, since it is based on a recognition and legitimisation of the presence of others in the learning relationship. It requires a grounding in technological skills but also the ability to support a narrative, dialogic architecture of online participation. It is, therefore, closely related to appreciative reflection and reflective learning processes (Ghaye et al., 2008).

Appreciative stewardship consists of the activity of fostering the development and improvement of individual visions expressed in various forms; for example narrative, of giving them a voice and a representation, and of bringing them together in order to co-construct a bigger, dynamic and collective vision.

The 'leader steward' is not the owner of the organisation in which he/she works, the financial and human resources he/she uses, or the visions he/she helps to construct. Similarly, the appreciative steward's power of action is 'limited' to responsibility for representing, communicating and putting into action the various individual visions and organising them in a collective vision, but with some additional aspects/responsibilities:

(1) constructing the context and relationship conditions that enable all participants to take part and express themselves freely;
(2) encouraging the valorisation of the positive, achievable aspects of individual visions and attempting not to be led into dilemmas with no possible solutions, or into conflictual dynamics;
(3) fostering the co-construction of a collective awareness or wisdom and, therefore, passing from a vision focusing on the individual to one focusing on the group or community;

(4) organising a collective vision with respect to which the development of the group and of individuals is planned and sustainable; and
(5) encouraging a shared construction of meaning with respect to action and to acting in the direction decided upon.

The reflective learning considered here is based on an appreciative reflection. It refers to a type of reflective thought that aims to identify, valorise and transform/expand the scope of meaning that is most appropriate for a given group of participants and to emphasise the conditions in which it occurs. This is an intentional process, whose social context is of a fundamental importance and within which the experience of the individual participants and of the group is recognised and valued. It is a process within which participants are not just users but active participants whose objective is learning, transformation and improvement – individual, of the group and of the organisation.

References

Amin, A., & Roberts, J. (2006, August). Communities of Practices? Varieties of Situated Learning, paper presented at EU Network of Excellence Dynamics of Institutions and Markets in Europe (DIME), Durham, UK.

Berge, Z., & Collins, M. (1996). *Facilitating interaction in computer mediated online courses, FSU/AECT distance education conference.* Retrieved from http://jan.ucc.nau.edu/~mpc3/moderate/flcc.html.

Dubé, L., Bourhis, A., & Jacob, R. (2003). Towards a tipology of virtual communities of practice, *Chaiers du GreSI,* n.03–13, Montreal: HEC.

Ghaye, T., Melander-Wikman, A., Kisare, M., Chambers, P., Bergmark U., Kostenius, C., & Lillyman, S. (2008). Participatory and appreciative action and reflection (PAAR). Democratizing reflective practices. *Reflective Practice, 9*(4), 361–397.

Gherardi, S. (2008). Dalla comunità di pratica alla pratica delle comunità: breve storia di un concetto in viaggio [From communities of practice to practices of community], *Studi Organizzativi,* 1.

Gherardi, S., & Bruni, A. (2007). *Studiare le pratiche lavorative* [Studying working practices]. Bologna: Il Mulino.

Jacobs, G. (2006). Imagining the flowers, but working the rich and heavy clay: Participation and empowerment in action research for health. *Educational Action Research, 14*(4), 569–581.

Latour, B. (2002). *Le fabrique du droit, La fabbrica del diritto* [The firm of rights]. Città Aperta: Enna.

Phillips, A. (1995). *The politics of presence.* Oxford: Oxford University Press.

Schön, D. (1983). *The reflective practitioner. How professionals think in action.* New York: Basic Books.

Senge, P. (1998). The practice of innovation. *Leader to Leader, 5*(9) section 2.

Sfard, A. (1998). On two metaphor for learning and the danger of choosing just one. *Educational Researcher, 27*(2), 4–13.

Shirky, C. (2003, April). A group is its own worst enemy: Social structure in social software. Paper presented at the O'Reilly Emerging Technology conference, Santa Clara, CA, April 2003. http://www.shirky.com/writings/group_enemy.html.

Suchman, L.A., Blomberg, J., Orr, J.E., & Trigg, R. (1999). Reconstructing technologies as a social practice. *American Behavioural Scientist, 43*(3), 392–408.

Turkle, S. (1995). *Life on the screen: Identity in the age of the internet.* New York, Simon & Schuster.

Wenger, E., White, N., & Smith, J.D. (2009). *Digital habitats. Stewarding technologies for communities.* Portland, OR: Cpsquare.

Reflection on building appreciative memory

Elisa Cavicchiolo[a,b] and Simona Marchi[a,b]

[a]*Department of Economics, 'Sapienza' University of Rome, Rome, Italy;* [b]*Reflective Learning Italy, Rome, Italy*

The pathways embarked upon in a reflective practice approach presuppose a constant focus on the narratives, processes and shifts that occur along the way. These elements are not always expressed and do not always become objects for systematic reflection. The risk, for both participants and facilitators, is that of losing the sense of the lived experience. The need to avoid losing the memory of these events and to enhance and build upon them led us progressively to an awareness of the need for a new instrument that would help us in this work of archiving and developing stories, processes and shifts that we were experiencing as participants and facilitators within an EU-founded project called Reflect-OR. The dimensions that this instrument has enabled us to explore concerned the development of an appreciative memory, a way of representing experience and creating a space for relationships that remains stable over time. We called this weaving/mapping instrument – which in effect consisted of more than one instrument – *reléchange*.

'What could I bring away with me from that story? While at the same time trying not to lose my own stories along the way, because I realised that at the beginning I was struggling to remember all the things that had happened, maybe some of these stories could help us to progress a little, to evolve our work'.

Figure 1. Reflection of participant.

Introduction

In the practice of reflection, various tools are used to encourage the development of individual and group pathways for reflection, both during and/or after the action (Stroobants, Chamber, & Clarke, 2007). These instruments are designed to foster reflection on lived experience or the creation of a new experience and can be based on storytelling and/or writing (traditional and digital/electronic).

Meta-reflection on these pathways is often achieved through a facilitator, who can assume different roles within and out with the organisation in which the pathways are conducted (trainer, in-house teacher, human resources development officer, external consultant, colleague). These few steps have certain implicit features: the organisational context is a given; roles are clear; the system of rules is, as far as possible, set out; the professional qualifications, division of labour and career pathways are clearly defined, as are the goals, method and instruments. So what is going wrong?

Our experience, as described in this paper, is part of a European innovation transfer project. The aim, therefore, is the transfer of an innovation, represented by a certain methodological approach, with a view to encouraging a certain type of process of reflection on professional practice (in this case the methodology is both the means and the end). The organisational context under consideration is the one generated by the project itself: an interorganisational temporary organization (cf., in this special issue, *PAAR-Time. The relationship between temporary and non-temporary organizations in the development of participatory, appreciative action, learning and reflection experiences*), or *Two or more non-temporary organizations collaborating to accomplish a joint task with the duration of the collaboration explicitly* ex-ante *fixed either by a specific date or by the attainment of a predefined task or condition* (Keni, Janowicz-Panjaitan, & Cambré, 2009, p. xiv).

While the project's goal is innovation transfer and the organisational context has the characteristics set out above, we fully realise that the organisational cultures of the non-temporary organisations under consideration tend to be much stronger than any intervention, external or internal, designed to promote innovation. Unless, that is, the intervention is structured more as a process of adoption from outside and less as an individual and organisational learning process (Consoli, 2002).

The need developed in the course of various reflective practice experiences, including the one relevant to the Reflect-OR project, to identify ways through which the verbal and oral narratives produced within reflection pathways could be made consistent, persistent and resistant to the inertia and routines produced by the organisational culture concerned.

The idea was to construct recognisable narrative spaces with their own specific identity within the project pathways and organisations concerned. Within these spaces, the narratives should be able to go on existing and developing. This need, linked to the question of innovation, understood as a learning pathway, means, first and foremost, acknowledging the double power of the innovative method: that of fostering the innovation and stabilisation of that same method:

> The narrative mode enables us to make concurrent and multiple reconstructions/representations of the world since its validation criterion is plausibility. Indeed, it is through narration that a situation acquires meaning for oneself and for others because it is by narrating that we construct the categories that give a name and a meaning to the events narrated. In reality, the extraordinary power of narrative knowledge lies in the link which people establish, through narrations, between the exceptional and the ordinary, when

> they attempt to establish explanations, justifications and interpretations of common everyday facts. (Czarniawska, 1997, p. ix)

This double movement of the narrative mode – the innovation and stabilisation of practices – does not occur automatically. It is, rather, a process that must be co-managed by a group of participants and the traces of its effects should be sought in narrative empirical evidence. They should be exploited and made legible and intelligible.

As part of the European Reflect-OR project, we attempted to build new methods through which to keep track of this movement, the component parts of which are represented by the movements of individual and group narratives. We called this method *reléchange.*[1] The idea of using the word *reléchange* is to indicate the restitution pathway as created in the Reflect-OR workshops. This arose from the need to find the most comprehensive term possible to bring out the different angles of the restitution process.

On the one hand, the word *reléchange* underscores the idea of change, one of the pillars of the PAAR process. In this sense, reléchange 'monitors' change, takes into account the evolution of the individual and of the working group, conveys an understanding of how far we have come, where we started from and how far we can go. And on the other hand, the word draws on the meaning given by Senge (Senge, 1998) to the verb 'to relate'. *Reléchange* is, therefore, not as a simple collection of stories told, but is an elaboration that helps us to give a meaning to those stories and to learn from the stories within our own living and working environments, at both the individual and group level.

Reléchange, however, also evokes a French term, *relais*, which, before the advent of cars, stood for each of the stations where the mail coaches could change their tired horses. The term was later transferred to the telegraphy field, where it stood for the devices that enabled messages in Morse code to be transmitted from one station to the next.

Reléchange was conceived with this spirit in an attempt to encapsulate the reflections, stories and ideas created by and emerging from the group and transferring them to paper without losing the sense of the path travelled, the creativity of that path, and the individual and collective moments encountered upon it. It was an operation, therefore, not merely of recording meetings. There was always an attempt to give something more, to re-transmit to the station of departure all the richness of the original message, enhanced by new impulses, new food for thought, new ways of saying things, so that the restitution would always act as the starting point for the next meeting:

> Alongside the role of facilitator the critical importance of the role of the 'restorer' emerged, as a positive figure. Normally, at the end of the meetings we produced agendas and to-do lists. But these do not restore what really happened, the added value of space B with respect to space A. This method enables not just continuity but also a development, a narrative; it introduces a specific viewpoint. It is a less charismatic role than that of facilitator, but one that is probably more innovative.
>
> Reflection by a CIOFS project participant (see Figure 1)

In this paper we will take into account this *reléchange* construction/weaving and the meaning it has acquired at three levels: individual, group and organisational (within each context and project), in light of the meta-reflection characteristics generated.

Reléchange: a kind of storytelling between memory and change

In 2009, the journal *Organization* published a special issue dedicated to the relationship between storytelling and change, entitled *Storytelling and change: An unfolding story* (Brown, Gabriel, & Gherardi, 2009). In the introduction to the issue, the storytellers wrote that from a review of the literature on the topic, storytelling practices appear to be non-linear and to belong to different, fragmented, distributed and collective themes. These are all insights that have contributed to research on, and theories of, change in organizations and processes of organising (Brown & Jones, 1998; Currie & Brown, 2003).

The close connections between storytelling and change research have frequently been observed (Barry & Elmes, 1997; Carr, 1986; Humphreys & Brown, 2002a, 2002b). The editors go on to state that both storytelling and the research on the subject of change have at their core the notion of temporality and are intended to describe, understand and explain complex processes in which different actors act in different contexts, which unfold in conditions of uncertainty and ambiguity:

> Whether stories are interpreted as constituting, mapping, encouraging, managing, upsetting, preventing or inviting change, they are an ever present feature of patterns of becoming, always evocative of actual futures and possible worlds. They are the means by which executives manage and the disaffected resist, they inhabit the boardroom and the unmanaged interstitial spaces in which those effected by power express their fantasies and their disquiet. Stories are, often concomitantly, aids to memory and ways of forgetting, diagnostic tools and distractions, means for social control and expressions of liberation, hegemonic and subversive. In all these ways, and others, stories are key to our conceptions, theories and research on change. (Brown, Gabriel, & Gherardi, 2009, p. 325)

Reléchange responds to the need to adopt a different point of view to encourage a different representation of the process and of the individual contributions produced through creative storytelling. A standpoint that is not external to the 'reality' of the situation but that is not internal either to the human mind, that is neither merely objective nor merely subjective, merely quantitative or merely qualitative. It springs, therefore, from the attempt to offer a mobile, process-driven point of view. The epistemological assumption is that of considering lived experience in the context of the Reflect-OR project. A project made up of actors, cultures, actions and relationships, as the fruit of continuous interactions between its component elements, in which the tensions between individualisation and differentiation, on the one hand, and adoption and participation on the other, assume forms that are not entirely known or foreseeable.

In complex systems that are configured to provide answers to increasingly complex questions (from the world of guidance and outplacement in times of economic crisis to care services for the elderly to high-reliability systems, and so on), what is produced through social interactions becomes the strategic yet mobile element of organisational systems as well as the force constantly driving those systems to question themselves. From the field of medicine, to IT, to social services, and even to dance, practitioners increasingly find themselves having to address the 'uniqueness' and 'complexity' of situations for action that involve a continuous rethinking of the processes, instruments and modes of planning, selection and action. In this relationship of uniqueness with respect to the object, which is at the same time critical and strategic, professional knowledge is put to the test by the complexity of practical situations. What place does all this have in organisations?

This uniqueness seems to break into the relationship between practitioner and the object of the professional action whenever we see a growth in demand for quality in all spheres of life, including those of knowledge-production. This increase in demand for quality occurs when the 'client', 'user', 'stakeholder' or 'citizen' becomes the object of an overturning of the relationships between practitioners and beneficiaries and becomes part of the process of defining needs, designing the product/service and evaluating its efficacy. The 'client' becomes the object of a reflective project through which organisations and practitioners redefine their decision-making processes, practices and identities. This is even stronger in the new professions or non-regulated occupations such as the world of guidance counselling, for which competition and the free market place the client at the centre of their strategic and identity-related decisions more than is the case in the traditional professions and occupations.

This change places the complexity of the objects of the professional action in the foreground and opens up to discussion the relationship between the practitioner, the object of his or her action, and knowledge and the way it is constructed, exchanged, recognised and shaped in specific organisational contexts. But above all it brings into question the professional relationships between actors with expert knowledge and actors with other knowledge, and imposes a need to rethink artefacts, knowledge, processes and activities. Professional experience increasingly becomes synonymous with the capacity to intervene in situations perceived as 'difficult', 'unprecedented', 'peculiar' or 'innovative', or to act in situations in which 'minority relationships' occur to which lower probability estimates are associated and in which actions are taken in conditions of great uncertainty. Within these processes, action becomes dense with investments (emotional, cognitive, strategic) and is capable of creating its own meanings (Melucci, 1998; Schön, 1983).

Reléchange is based on a different approach to storytelling: one that is designed to build upon a specific type of narrative; a positive narrative that is appreciative and open to change. This construction is based on the narration of a particular type of individual experience. Those perceived by practitioners as positive and successful, albeit unprecedented, episodes that have sprung from singular, difficult situations with the goal of favouring their memory and helping develop the ability to remember not just negative but positive episodes too. We have seen that the construction of an appreciative narrative space requires a specific timescale, the timescale necessary for the development of an appreciative memory and a lexicon open to development and the opening up of stories. *Reléchange* envisages the creation of a collective weaving/mapping of the stories narrated and reflections developed individually and in groups. This weaving/mapping is able to take into account at one and the same time any peculiarities and specific contextual and recurrent aspects, and is intended to co-construct a collective positive narrative knowledge.

Scientific thought and its reporting methods developed through an attempt to de-subjectify knowledge and objectify the world, producing dualisms such as the separation of subject and reality, observer and observed reality, observing system and system observed and defining as scientific that knowledge produced through specific protocols of study, observation, description, analysis, synthesis and communication. Such protocols confer certain characteristics such as objectivity (i.e. transparency) and free it from the actor or actors producing it and from the specific context in which it is produced. Reflective narrative thought (Cortese, 1999) tries, instead, to overcome these dualisms, and therefore bridge the divide between 'observer and observed', 'subject and object', 'quantity and quality'. It lays the foundations for a process-based, circular knowledge based on systems of continuous retro-action between subjects, contexts and instruments, considering social reality as a reflective construction that occurs through these relationships, including the intervention of the trainer/facilitator.

A central question in the development of *reléchange* is the identification of pertinent methodologies and techniques with respect to individual organisational contexts and situations.

Reléchange in the Reflect-OR project: experience, discovery and lessons learned

The *reléchange* narrative within the Reflect-OR project is intended to reflect the spirit of discovery and learning-by-doing that has characterised the progressive inclusion of restitution in the reflection on operators' practice. We therefore had the idea of structuring this section as if it were an interview, seeking to bring out through few, but significant, questions, the sense and meaning that *reléchange* has had in our project's pathway made of several workshops in person. At certain points of the interview we decided to insert participants' reflections that were important to us in acquiring an awareness of the sense and use of *reléchange*. The figures we decided to include during the interview provide an example of the method and style of the *reléchange*. At the end of each of the questions we showed a word-cloud that makes it possible, in our opinion, to establish the key elements of the discourse. The decision to use the interview format arose from an underlying idea that has guided us in constructing this article: the interview is at one and the same time a method for developing a conversation on the meaning of lived experiences and a way to lead people to reflect (van Manen, 1990):

> First question: How was the idea of building an instrument different from the usual form of report born?

The idea was born from the need to find a narrative language that would enable us to recount what guidance counselling practitioners were experiencing. We asked ourselves how we could visualise the pathway, track the path we were following, stone after stone – *reléchange* after *reléchange* – with its ups and downs, its diversions, it own signposts and landmarks. We realised how important it was to reflect on the stories being told and the elements we were learning during the meetings not only 'there and then', at the end of the day, but over time, retracing after each meeting the road we had followed. And so we thought *reléchange* could provide the opening for each meeting, a time for reflection in which we said: what stage are we at? What did we say to each other last time? What pathway are we following?:

> What could I take away with me from that story? While at the same time trying not to lose my own stories along the way, because I realised that at the beginning I was struggling to remember all the things that had happened, maybe some of these stories could help us to progress a little, to evolve our work.
>
> Reflection by a project participant from the Chamber of Commerce system

A first element we feel should be underlined is this need to not lose the component parts of the pathway, to trace out an *appreciative and participatory memory* of the experience. But what do we mean by appreciative and participatory memory? How is a memory of this type constructed? The value of written memory is acquired with the passing of time. Whenever an episode that is significant to us occurs, it seems impossible

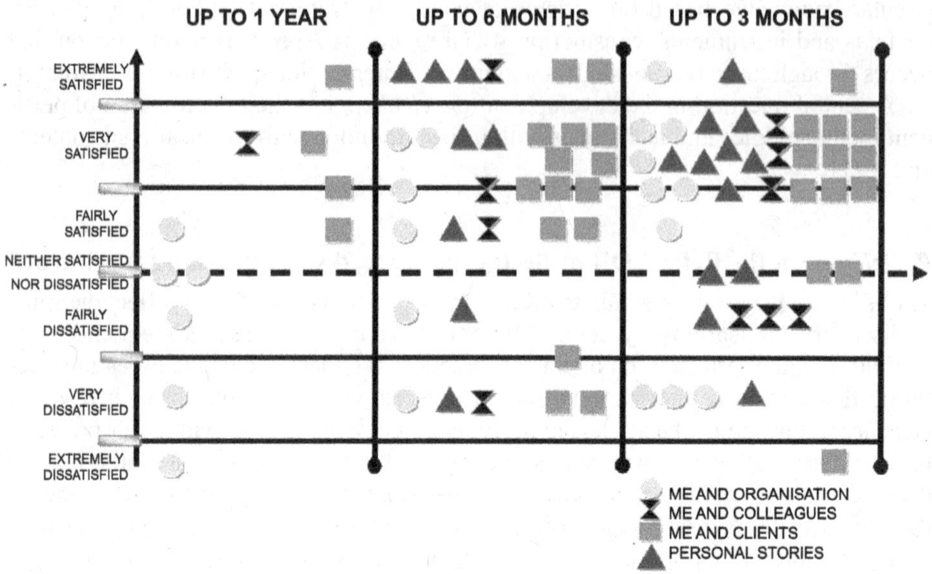

Figure 2. The satisfaction curve to understand what types of stories give us and others a sense of well-being.
Notes: Figure 2 shows a tool called 'the satisfaction curve'. The curve, made at the individual level and then returned at the group level, archives the stories according to the degree of satisfaction or well-being that this story gave to the participants. It also takes into account the temporal dimension and the classification showed in Figure 3 (me and organization/colleagues/clients). The satisfaction curve is a tool which helps people to think on their experience, to reflect on what episodes made them feeling good and what made them feeling not such well. At the collective level it helps to understand in which areas there is a high number of positive stories, where they are located in the curve and it helps to investigate the reasons for choosing that particular story.

that we will forget those details; lose sight of the reasons that led us to act in that way; not remember the exact order of events. As we gradually accumulate significant events, we increasingly struggle to distinguish the specific elements of each story, the story is turned into a slogan – often a negative one such as 'don't trust' or 'the only person you can rely on is yourself'. We lose the complexity of the event, its wealth of details. In this respect, *reléchange* helped us to construct an *archive of stories and processes*, to develop a positive memory of the individual and group pathway that had been laid down and followed.

The *appreciative* nature of this construction lies in the progressive awareness that learning stories does not just mean retaining the memory of your *own* stories. It also means giving value to the contribution made by others' experience. The development of an appreciative eye was one of the key elements distinguishing the entire pathway (cf., in this Special Issue, *Co-constructing an appreciative collective eye. Voices from Reflect-OR project experience*). *Reléchange* was most certainly one of the vehicles for this important learning experience (Figure 2). The *participatory* nature of this type of memory emerges transparently from *reléchange*. There is a continuous alternation between individual and collective moments of reflection, between stories that start from the experience of the individual and are transformed through maps or diagrams into moments of reflection and learning for the entire group (Figure 3). The possibility of moving harmoniously from the individual to the collective dimension enables the group to develop a wisdom which is located at one and the same time at the individual and collective level and which affects the relationship with each actor's own professional role, with the organisation, with colleagues and with users.

Alongside this element linked to the development of an appreciative participatory memory, we feel we should underscore that in our pathway, *reléchange* also played an important role as a tool for reflection on the process. At the beginning of each of our Reflect-OR meetings, participants had an opportunity to retrace the road followed thus far, to lay down the common thread (*fil rouge*) of the process, to reconsider the experience narrated by the stories – thus introducing an experience re-framing dimension (see Figure 4). We told the operators several times that restitution was the snapshot of a moment in which a certain type of story had been told, in a certain context, in a certain individual, group and organisational time span. It was therefore necessary to rethink and retrace the experience that emerged from the stories to understand how to follow the pathway and what actions-for-change should be brought into play. We left *empty spaces* in the restitutions in which ideas, reflections and comments could be included. The aim here was to convey the idea that the process did not end the moment the restitution was handed back, but that, rather, it started again at that very

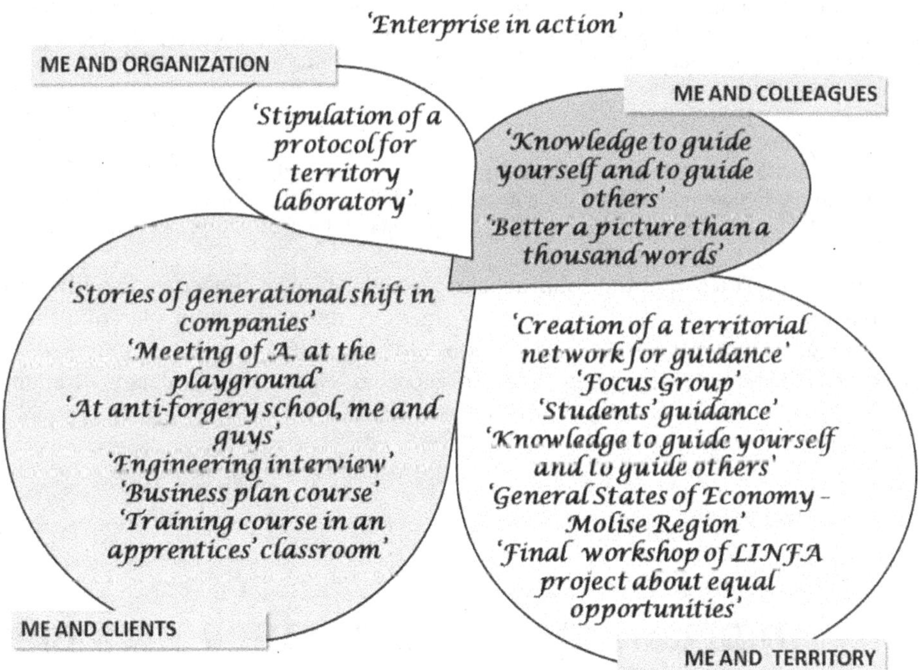

Figure 3. Classification of the group's stories by four areas of reference. Another way to understand what to reflect on.
Notes: Figure 3 represents a collection of stories of a working group. We have chosen, throughout the whole project, to highlight some significant indicators related to the role and to the profession of guidance workers, such as me and organization, me and colleagues, me and clients. The classification has allowed us to go deeper in each of these chosen themes.

moment, as though the facilitator were once again throwing the ball back into the operator's court.

In our pathway it was not important whether the time when the experience was rethought was or was not interspersed by 'in-person' meetings with the practitioners. Indeed, *reléchange* was both a support tool for immediate reflection and an instrument to consult, rediscover and rethink over time. In this respect, we were struck by a comment by one of the participants:

> I didn't look at the restitutions from one meeting to the next. However, when we got to the end of the process I felt the need to go back, to retrace our steps through those same restitutions.
>
> Reflection by an ECAP project participant

> Second question: Has *reléchange* been a useful tool only to practitioners or for you as facilitators too?

Reléchange was and is a learning tool for all of us. While on the one hand it enabled participants to follow the common thread of the process, for us as project facilitators it was most definitely a tool for *coordination* and *monitoring*. We want to start from two brief narratives:

> The role of restitution also had a coordination effect, of weaving and unravelling (Penelope in reverse[2]), of focusing on the contribution made by each – including their contribution to the contribution made by each. This put right – in a discreet way – the latency that was felt at one point.
>
> Reflection by a CIOFS project participant

> I experienced this very much as a gift that gave me access to the common thread, which enabled me to continue beyond the contractual definition of the project.
>
> Reflection by a CIOFS project participant

One of the critical questions that accompanied this project concerned the difficulty of constructing a participatory appreciative memory during the time span of a European project, i.e. two years (cf., in this special issue, *Temporariness in appreciative reflection*). How to maintain the idea of a process when the 'in-person' training

Figure 4. Key words that emerged underling the key elements from the first question.

moments are chronologically distant? In a reflection pathway of this type, conceived and designed to be a continuum, albeit one that in practice follows the rhythm imposed by specific events and meetings, the facilitators' role of coordinating the process becomes complicated and often risks proceeding unevenly, with participation peaks in the run-up to the 'in-person' meetings and troughs in the intervals between them. Even though these intervals provide a space in which to reflect and to rethink the process, an important factor both for facilitators and for guidance counselling practitioners, they can instead be interpreted as a lack of coordination (as indeed they sometimes are) or lack of interest on the part of facilitators in the dynamics of the participants:

> 'The reason why I personally liked the pathway proposal is that it gave me a guarantee almost immediately that we would work under close-counselling arrangements. To some extent, all reflective practices require you to reflect on the experience without presuming to bring in content from outside. As you know, there is nothing more irritating for a trainer than to be given obligatory content in a training project. We also like to work on building the training requirement rather than on the content itself [Figure 5]. It is good to be involved with the projects on which we intend to work. So a structured, clear and fairly strong method as procedure – which, however, is used taking content that emerges entirely from the group as a starting point.
>
> Reflection by an Ecap project participant

In this respect, *reléchange* is a coordination aid, a sort of *invisible coordination tool* that is able to maintain the common thread of the process and the stability of the relationship, even during the intervals or when there is a lack of proper coordination – which can happen even in the presence of the facilitators.

The second key question concerned the monitoring and evaluation of a PAAR process. How can I monitor the learning of a PAAR process? How can I evaluate whether or not learning has taken place? There is no lack of monitoring and assessment tools in the training field, but they rarely succeed in encapsulating the idea of process. Very often they are an evaluation, a reflection on a learning experience in a given place and at a given time, too easily influenced by the external environment, by the individual's emotions and above all too much 'in the moment' rather than 'between the moments'.

As the narratives of this pathway have taught us, the effort to monitor and reconstruct the learning process is not something that facilitators alone – who are responsible for providing the output material of the project or group pathway – take upon themselves. It is also an explicit request by the participants who find themselves, when they reach the end of a pathway, with a need to understand what they have learned and to themselves monitor the change that has taken place. In this respect, *reléchange* allowed us to focus continuously on the little stones making up our path. It teased out elements of monitoring and evaluation directly from participants' experience and stories without the need to import external survey tools or define the role of evaluator and evaluated.

Another learning element for us as facilitators was to learn to *represent the experience* of a project hinging on reflective practices – on something, therefore, that is difficult to represent. We tried to do this first of all through style (Figure 7). The restitutions indeed sought to maintain the spirit and sensations produced during the meeting without adding any other elements, without intervening on the stories in an invasive manner, but merely reshaping the reflections within a clear

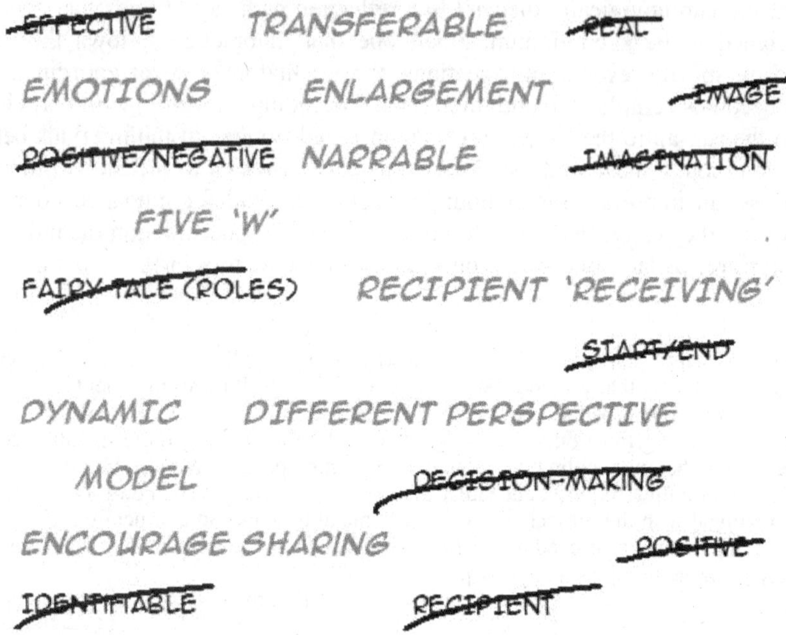

Figure 5. Identifying the elements of the stories that the group wants to tell through a selection/deletion process.
Notes: Figure 5 illustrates the process that led the participants to select the elements of the stories they wanted to tell. To choose some significant elements of a story gives an identity to the stories both at the individual and collective level. Through a process of elimination / selection, the participants defined what kind of stories they would tell the group. The process of constructing the panel of significant elements made us reflect on the meaning of a story as individuals, as practitioners and as a group.

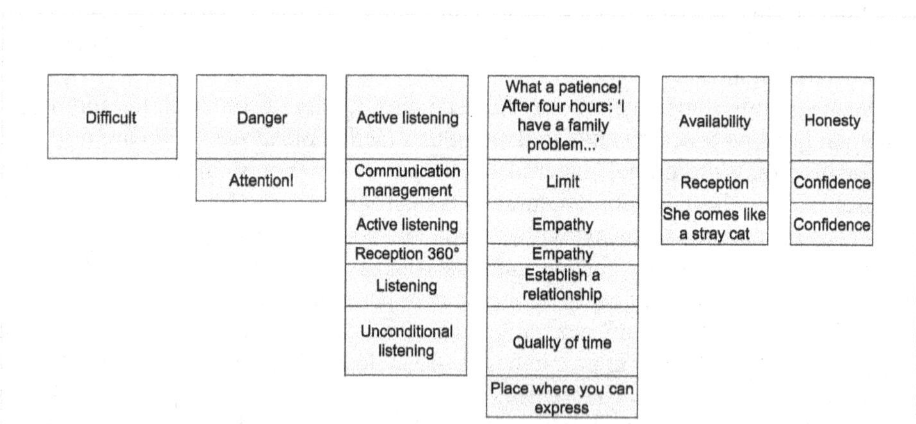

Figure 6. The emotional elements that emerged from the stories organised as post-its of key words and areas.
Notes: Figure 6 shows a way of representation of the issues raised by the stories of the group. Through the identification of keywords we have photographed and mapped, as in this case, the emotional elements of the stories. The mapping helped us to define not only the key elements of stories, but also the typical features of guidance workers' role and profession.

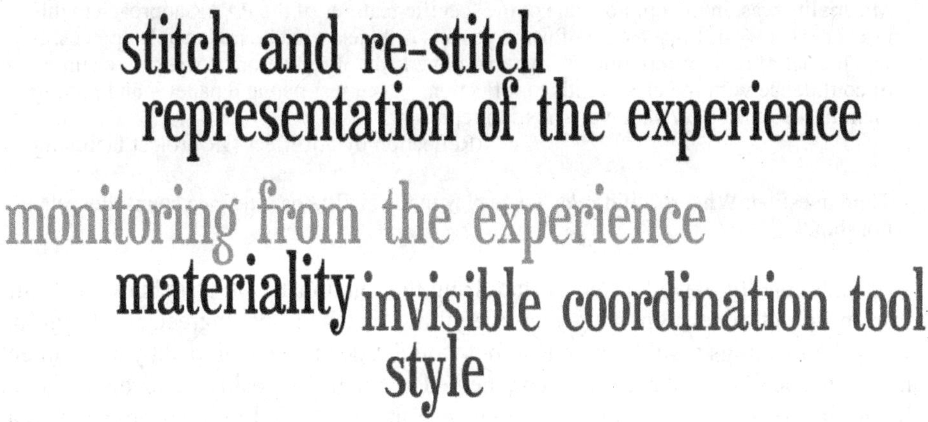

Figure 7. Key words that emerged underling the key elements from the second question.

methodological framework in such a way as to provide a different perspective of the things said. We were interested in bringing out the materiality of our meetings with practitioners in *reléchange* also, by using images, diagrams, post-its, tag-clouds and so on (Figure 8).

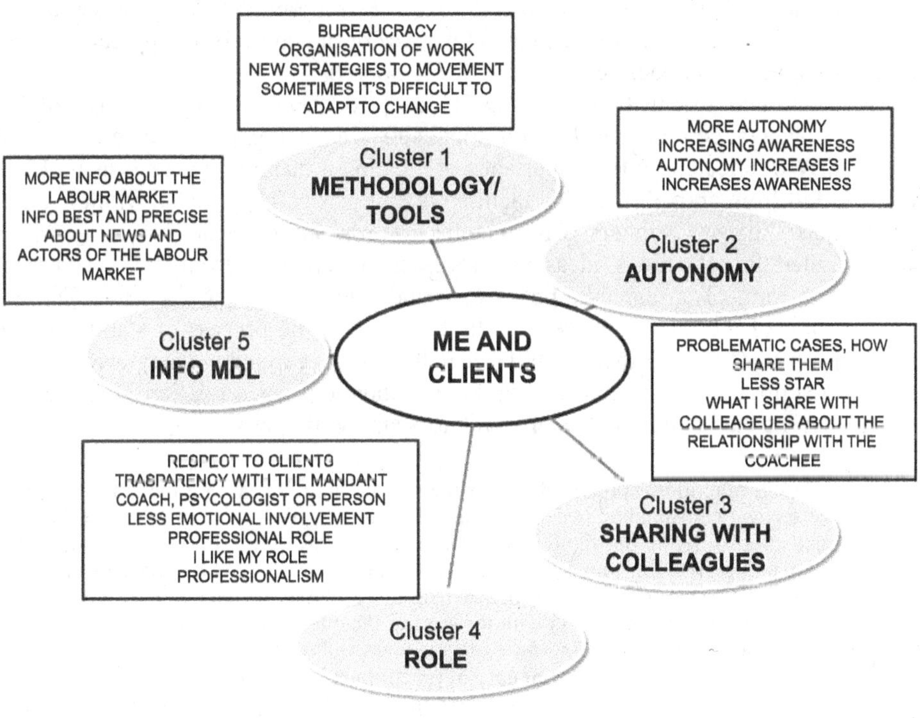

Figure 8. Stories of 'Me in relation to the client' grouped by macro-area to help identify areas of change.
Notes: Figure 8 explores the episodes related to one of the indicators considered in the path (me and clients). The group, through a process of keywords' grouping, defined the themes they needed to work on during the project, highlighting areas where it was necessary to develop reflection and a deeper dialogue between guidance practitioners.

> Materiality was, in my opinion, one of the specific features of the PAAR approach in this project. This wasn't just a case of using post-its or black/whiteboards or felt-tip pens. It was the act of re-appropriating the material dimension of reflection. It was the regaining of confidence with the classic aids to reflection – even just pen and paper – and putting them to the service of what we wanted to represent.
>
> Reflection by a Reflect-OR project facilitator

Third question: What role did *reléchange* play in the facilitator-guidance counsellor relationship?

It undoubtedly played a role in stabilising the relationship of trust between facilitator and practitioner. Knowing that everything that had been agreed by the group during the meetings would not be lost, but would indeed be developed by a document and by a specific explanatory event, helped maintain a positive and appreciative climate in the group. It is sometimes the case in story-based training processes that participants get an impression of 'donating' their experience, including their emotional experiences, to the facilitator without actually taking part in a true exchange, as though they were not getting anything in return for their gift.

This message could then be picked up in an even more extreme manner by interpreting the learning as a one-way street going from facilitator to participant, with no return path. But if each of the moments, stories and reflections that are born from the process are restored to participants, the feeling is no longer one of an extortion. It is, rather, one of a *shared and agreed and ethical construction of meaning*, based on the awareness of being able to relate in a 'safe' space designed to foster appreciativeness and a democratic approach (cf. *Reflect-OR Fieldbook*).

An important moment in this respect occurred during the initial stage of the project, when a context analysis questionnaire was being prepared, created and returned. We reflected on the importance of creating a quantitative analysis tool that did not 'fall from above', from the facilitators, but was co-constructed with the guidance counselling practitioners. This was the first *reléchange* in our project in which we restituted the reflections, ideas and processes that emerged from this co-construction in the form of an agreed, appreciative and truly useful questionnaire. The co-construction of the questionnaire was the first step in the process of stabilising the relationship since it made their central role in the project explicit to the guidance counselling practitioners. In so doing, it laid the foundations for a relationship based on trust, listening and sharing between facilitators and participants:

> Some CIOFS practitioners thanked me for the questionnaire because it made them feel they were being consulted on two things they deem to be very important. The first, how important it is to define the figure, the role, to 'place' the figure, to give recognition, while remaining free from any talk of professional associations and orders. And the second, to have been questioned on their perception of the work. They greatly appreciated this type of questionnaire. As with the stories, the questionnaire can also develop a methodological pointer indicating how questionnaires should develop: brief, focused, hinging on the key points for this category of practitioners. A shared and agreed process, with the questionnaire developed not by institutions but by people who actually do this job. Simplification, reduction, to succeed in hitting the target.
>
> Reflection by a CIOFS project participant

Another important point, which is linked to the comments already made on coordination, is connected with the difficulty of maintaining a relationship of trust over time. A relationship in which just a few meetings take place in person and which

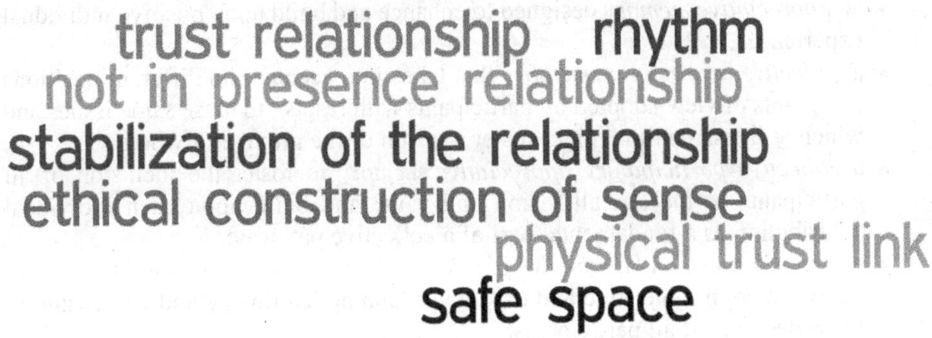

Figure 9. Key words that emerged underling the key elements from the third question.

unfolds, almost entirely, in the intervals between one meeting and another, through telephone conversations or emails:

> One of the aspects I appreciated in the project was the rhythm and pace, always well-spaced. We had about ten meetings, including with the trainers from the Rome team, in a year, and yet this was perhaps the first project I've taken part in that managed to keep us, all things considered, fairly active in the inter-session periods. I mean, we kept ourselves busy, the rhythms for 're-processing' were there, the timing was right for reflection. Sometimes we used these intervening periods well, sometimes we could have used them even better. But things really did move forward even in the inter-session periods.
>
> Reflection by an Ecap project participant

The participation format in our experience was characterised not just by the difficulty of combining events in person and periods 'at a distance', but also by the attempt to stabilise a relationship between a team of facilitators that alternates during the process and participants who could vary from one meeting to the next. *Reléchange* was also for us a useful tool to stabilise this type of complex relationship by forming a *physical bond of trust* between participants and facilitators (see Figure 9).

Conclusions

The idea of *reléchange* came into being in the context of the Reflect-OR project. It was based on a need initially, and above all, perceived by facilitators, to identify creative and participatory modalities to build a meta-narrative over the entire duration of the project, such as might foster a good balance between the need to build a collective memory of the process and the need to encourage innovation transfer. At the end of the project we can say that it was much more than this. As always happens, the participants, contexts and situations gave added dimensions to the initial need we identified and gave rise to a constant reformulation of their and our mutual expectations. They made it possible for *reléchange* to become a creative, co-constructed activity.

This activity made it possible to co-construct:

- the *memory* of each meeting and the individual and group reflections developed in it;

- an *appreciative memory* designed to enhance and build upon positive individual experiences;
- a *collective appreciative memory* that takes into account the different positions and points of view adopted by participants with respect to these same issues and which at the same time might foster a vision of the group as a whole;
- a *collective participatory appreciative memory* to foster the inclusion of all participants in the overall vision and value and build upon each individual contribution as a fundamental part of a collective pathway;
- a *shared, agreed and distinctive physical narrative space, a space for 'us'* with its own recognisable style and capable of lending legitimacy and citizenship to the reflections of all participants;
- an *incremental narrative space* that is capable of welcoming and being enriched by all those new participants/facilitators who might join the pathway from one occasion to the next;
- a *bond of trust* in which, in addition to reflections, stories and emotions, and the body too, the physical nature of words and space, facial expressions, the representation of doing as it is being done, are brought into play;
- a *group, individual and process assessment tool with respect to the project goals, a tool also to coordinate* the activities carried out by the facilitators, when these are different; and
- also to ensure the mappability of the pathway to foster *the possibility of moving lifelong and life-wide in reflection* with respect to the various points of the life-cycle of the experience lived together; in this sense, encourage processes for re-framing and the development of positive-action plans.

Notes

1. The concept of *reléchange/reléchanger* was coined and used for the first time by Annalisa Casino. A reference to the use of this term can be found in the reflections '*Chi è e cosa fa il leader as a steward – reléchange- reléchange n° 1: Essere o non essere*' posted by Annalisa Casino on the POILab blog (http://poilab.splinder.com/).
2. The sense of the assertion is the opposite of the traditional figure of Penelope. In the Odyssey Penelope, waiting for the return of her husband Ulysses, she didn't want to celebrate a new wedding. So every night she undid the cloth weaved during the day. In the same way, *reléchange* weaves time by time the story (the cloth) of our project's path.

References

Barry, D., & Elmes, M. (1997). Strategy Retold: Towards a Narrative View of Strategic Discourse, *Academy of Management Review 22*: 429–52.

Brown, A.D., Gabriel, Y., & S. Gherardi (2009). Storytelling and change: an unfolding story. *Organization, 16*(3): 323–333.

Brown, A. D., & Jones, M. (1998). Doomed to Failure: Narratives of Inevitability and Conspiracy in a Failed IS Project, *Organization Studies 19*(1): 73–88.

Carr, D. (1986). *Time, narrative and history*. Bloomington, IN: Indiana University Press.

Consoli, F. (2002). *Le mode professionali* [The professional fashion]. Roma: Carocci.

Cortese, G.C. (1999). *L'organizzazione si racconta* [The organizational storytelling]. Milano: Guerrini e Associati.

Currie, G., & Brown, A. D. (2003). A Narratological Approach to Understanding Processes of Organizing in a UK Hospital, *Human Relations 56*(5): 563–86.

Czarniawska, B. (1997). *Narrating the organization. Dramas of institutional identity,* trad. it., 2000. Torino: Edizioni di Comunità.

Ghaye, T., Alexandrov, A., Barile, A., Bednarz, F., Cavicchiolo, E., Consoli, F., et al. (forthcoming). *Orientamento partecipativo. Le pratiche riflessive per lo sviluppo della professionalità* [Participative and appreciative career guidance activities]. Roma: Carocci.

Humphreys, M., & Brown, A. D. (2002b). Dress and Identity: A Turkish Case Study, *Journal of Management Studies 39*(7): 929–54.

Humphreys, M., & Brown, A. D. (2002a). Narratives of Organizational Identity and Identification: A Case Study of Hegemony and Resistance, *Organization Studies 23*(3): 421–47.

Kenis, P., Janowicz-Panjaitan, M., & Cambré, M. (2009). *Temporary organizations. Prevalence, logic and effectiveness* (Massachussetts, USA, Edward Elgar Publishing).

Melucci, A., (1998). *Verso una sociologia riflessiva* [Towards a reflective society]. Bologna: il Mulino.

Schön, D. (1983). *The reflective practitioner: How professionals think in action* (NY, Basic Books).

Senge, P. (1998). 'The practice of innovation', *Leader to Leader, 5*(9): Section 2.

Stroobants, H., Chambers, P., & Clarke, B. (eds). (2007). *Reflective journeys: A fieldbook for facilitating life-long learning in vocational education and training*. Leuven: Acco.

van Manen, M. (1990). *Researching lived experience.* London: SUNY.

Facilitating capabilities through reflection: from welfare to appreciative well-being

Francesco Consoli

Department of Economics, 'Sapienza' University of Rome, Rome, Italy and Reflective Learning Italy, Rome, Italy

During the laboratories of the Reflect-OR project, the guidance counseling practitioners told some stories of success regarding their professional practice. From these stories a leitmotif emerges. In many cases the success is not solving the difficulty of a person (especially finding a new job, entering into a program of training etc.) but it is about facilitating a reframing process. Also, this success isn't the result of direct action but of giving the clients the opportunity and the experience necessary to understand their sustainable and real exigencies and to act appropriately. In this article I link the evidence of the changes in the professional practice of the guidance practitioners with the emergence of the concept of capability in a debate about justice and welfare. The guidance practitioners that were the protagonists of our laboratories in the Reflect-OR project became skilled in a very difficult tightrope walk. Born as professionals inside the welfare state institutions, they were shifting to a more counseling oriented mission. This is a radical change in the meaning and culture of their service, their profession and their relationship with clients, institutions and colleagues. The Reflect-OR project, with its participative appreciative action and reflection (PAAR) approach, has not only been able to detect such a shift, but it has also been able to give positive suggestions to increase the quality of the service and of the professional life.

1. From resources to capabilities

The concept of capabilities is from the early 1980s and is one of the most relevant ways to rethink justice, equity and equality as well as national accounting, public policies and welfare. However, the analysis of the economist Amartya Sen (2009), the political philosopher Martha Nussbaum (2000) and other scholars opened a new horizon not only to social sciences and to policy makers, but also to social workers and helping professions born in the frame of welfare state. Capability is a demanding concept. The approach based on capabilities is a shift from a welfare frame of social help to a well-being frame; from an economic and rational definition of resources, assets needs and choices to a more diversified nature of activities that gives rise to happiness, self-appreciation and respect (Sennett, 2003). The emphasis is placed on the importance of real freedom in the assessment of a person's advantage and on the individual differences concerning the ability to transform resources into valuable activities. One of the implications of this approach is to give attention not only to individual choices, but also to the strategies that give meaning to and shape these choices. Relevant strategies are a synthesis of behaviors, feelings, values, intentions, calculations and habits and take into account not only the resources and the abstract rationality of individual choices but also the capabilities and the situated relational system of the individuals and their biographies. Even the poorest and the weakest persons have a strategy that orients and gives a horizon to their actions, choices, or inaction and lack of choice. This approach is very close to the PAAR methodology, because, in the same way, it assumes peoples' right and ability to have a say in decisions that affect their livelihood and which claim to generate knowledge about them (Ghaye et al., 2008):

> The appreciative characteristic is critical because of the way some forms of action maintain a problem-oriented view of the world. In so doing they diminish the capacity of the participants to produce innovative ways of moving forward, demonstrating the use of their imagination, increasing participation and generating the necessary strength-based dialogued required for sustainable improvement. (Ghaye et al., 2008, pp. 368–369)

It may happen that a person has developed self-defeating behaviors and strategies, and needs help to learn and reflect upon his situated and concrete behaviors and strategies in order to see his daily life and practice from another point of view. It may also happen that the context of his strategy and sense-making changed in a drastic way (loss of one's job, a heavy grief, a divorce, a disease or an injury that reduced or strongly changed his capabilities). But still the focus must be on the ability of the person to be the actor of his own strategy. Arguably, empowerment starts from this acknowledgement of the value of the otherness and the success of the helping process is the emergence of this otherness in the helping relationship. A new semantic and thematic field is emerging for the helping and facilitating family of professions: capabilities, otherness/differences, freedom, value, respect, 'contextualism', situational ethics, appreciation and human flourishing.

The facilitating and helping role of the guidance practitioners is shifting from one of experts giving psychological and technical help to another one closer to counselor or life coach. But the resources and the institutional context they are inserted in are still anchored in a more traditional and welfare setting. This can create a contradiction between formal and latent agreements, tools, words and actions. From these contradictions stems the unexpected. But the unexpected is a value: first of all because it is a learning opportunity for the practitioner, and secondly, because it is a room for the client to express their voice. In some ways, we can say that the unexpected is a mark of 'success' in the helping relationship.

In recent years, social workers and helping professionals have been facing a very hard challenge and are coping with a deep contradiction and strong ethical dilemmas. On the one hand the economic, social and occupational crisis puts them on the front line against impoverishment, unemployment and loss of resources and opportunities of an increasing number of people. On the other one, the reduction of economic and institutional resources and the decrease of the opportunities strongly limit their ability to give people the help they need. Bigger pressure and less 'power', this contradiction is worsening the quality of their professional life and their satisfaction, frequently causing frustration, stress, loss of meaning and burn out. 'Sometimes we feel we are wasting our time' was an expression we frequently heard during our laboratories, while speaking about the relationship with the users of the public service.

During the laboratories we asked professionals to tell stories that, according to the PAAR methodology, should be especially positive stories: stories of success. One of the most interesting pieces of evidence regarding the meaning of 'success' and 'positivity' expressed by the stories they chose to tell related to the question 'When do you feel you really "succeeded"?' Of course, some of the stories have been of success because the guidance service has been able to match straight with the demand of the client. But in most cases the participants of the laboratories proposed examples of success or positive stories coming from the kingdom of the 'unexpected'. This was often the result of a complex process of negotiation and discovery. Furthermore, most of them recognized that the real and main contribution they could give to people was not to offer them resources such as information, contacts or material help in their behavior (such as writing a CV), but especially to help them understand what they really wanted and to act appropriately, offering an opportunity of attention, reflectivity and appreciation. The success of the help they offered was especially related with this reflecting and appreciative process. In other words, while the formal contract between them and the users was that of giving professional resources, the inner content of their job and the latent contract is that of reflexive counselors. In other terms, the 'unexpected' was the result of an internal contradiction of the role they're playing. What I contend is that the professional stress that the guidance practitioners suffer, expresses a deeper change in their daily practice that is partially in contrast with its general frame and context still embedded into the welfare institutions.

2. Some stories of the unexpected and success

The following stories have been told by practitioners from the *Centri per l'Orientamento al Lavoro* (COL) during a laboratory of the Reflect-OR project. The laboratory was devoted to produce positive stories about their relationship with their clients. All practitioners have been told to tell those stories in small groups and then the group was invited to choose one to tell in a plenary time, where the stories have been shared and discussed. The stories has been reproduced, written and distributed to the members of the laboratories in order to share the memory of the work made together.

This is the first story that opens the door to the unexpected. The success and positive aspect of it is its learning content. Its title is: 'Reflection and action'.

Reflection and action

> A colleague of mine was engaged in a interview with a client looking for a job. In that moment a company called my office saying: 'We urgently need to staff the call centre'. My colleague said that he would have done a screening in the database of available people and then he would have called back as soon as possible with a list of eligible people. He hung up the phone and...sure enough the proposal was rebounded to the youth, who answered: 'Yes, yes, it's okay, it's my profile'. The operator called the company back, saying he already had a name. He felt great because he had been able to get the answer right away, like a magic wand. Half an hour later, the company calls and tells the operator that the person indicated was no longer interested in the work and then my colleague went from a delusion of omnipotence to wanting to smash into the table. We are between the devil and the deep blue sea. On the one hand we need to manage the relationship with the user and the expectations of the companies. On the other one we try not to lose credibility in front of the enterprises. It's a story that happens often.

During the group discussion of the story a colleague remarked:

> The boy who was in front of you asking for help hadn't time to think about the request, but sought the help of the counselor and then he too was involved in a process in which he no longer could be critical. He didn't decode his request for help (which he stammered to the operator). 'It's like when parents are seeking employment for their son', another colleague said. 'There was no personal metabolism, the attempt fails'. In the relationship with the customer a moment between reflection and action is necessary!

The title of this story could be: 'Too much efficiency!' In this story the failure is a consequence of the involvement of the youth into a process (the action of the professional) 'in which he no longer could be critical'. By that I mean the boy felt inhibited in his quest for a help, without time for reflecting, for metabolizing the new opportunity and to express his real, perhaps confused, desire: without 'freedom'. He 'just stammered' and the mistake of the official was that of not interpreting and puzzling out this stammering. There is a passage in this story that must be underlined. When the boy claimed: 'Yes, yes, it's OK, this is my profile!' The profile is the professional tool that mediates between the 'demand' and the 'offer'. As Eymard-Duvernay and Marchal (1996) contended with their large research, the profile is a professional tool aiming to produce, with efficacy and efficiency, the judgment of competence that matches demand and offer. But in this case the match between demand and offer did not match with the strategy and motivations of the youth, which are left behind the stage. We could also title this story: 'A demand without a voice'.

Here is another story labeled by its proponent 'Redefining together'. The proponent was a lifelong career guidance practitioner.

Redefining together

> A person I am following is a girl who was kicked out of an insurance company. She gave the company 20 years of her life, and then she was thrown away. She had ended up in this company by chance. The break with this company allowed her to rethink her life. She wanted to work with children, and I wanted to know whether it was real or related to a teenage moment, because on the other hand she hadn't built her life, she had no children, and at 42 she was not engaged. We worked on this aspect, on the fact that she had chosen work she was not interested in. For me there was something that hit a wrong note: she wanted to get into social work, but it was not clear what she meant for social, whether she wanted to be a nurse or a psychologist or whatever. One day she sends me an email where she says she could not come to the meeting because she had to do a job interview. After a little while she comes back and tells me that it is true that she wants work with children, but she realizes that the road is too long for her, she doesn't feel like undertaking it. Then, I tell her that it doesn't have to be so long. I suggest for her to take a course for children's play centre practitioner so she can go to work after six months. Then I stopped for a moment. Either I'm falling into the trap that she's looking finally for a job she really likes, social work, with children and so on, or she wants something different. Indeed, even thanks to these meetings, I can find the time to stop and understand that although people come up with ideas that are unclear, we head towards the idea that is a little clearer, because it is the easiest one, thus we have the answer right away without analyzing the situation for a moment. Therefore I asked her why she had gone to a job interview. It turned out that work is crucial to her. She cannot do without it. I realized together with her that she could not make the orientation journey because she could not get to reflect in depth. For example we had a skills assessment (*bilan de compétence*): the family field was empty, the training load was empty, the work was 'yes'. In the end we redefined: At this moment you are not ready, you need more. But I do not think we should definitely close, there may be spaces. She's very good at working!

The process is expressed very clearly: 'Although people come up with ideas that are unclear, we head towards the idea that is a little clearer, because it is the easiest one, thus we give the answer right away without analyzing the situation for a moment'. The relationship between the client and the counselor is dialogical and based on a complex game of interactions through interviews, verbal games, explicit propositions and stories, technical tools (such as the *bilan de compétence*), information, proposals, actions and reactions, in a movement where the action and the 'no-action' (to give room to the client in order to express her/his implicit voice) are interwoven in a process of reciprocal interpretation. 'She is playing with the rules of the game but this doesn't correspond to her true motives'. This is a commentary to another story that can also be applied to this one: in fact, the relationship between the user and the lifelong career guidance practitioner is ambiguous because it is based on two kinds of agreement. The first one – explicit – is institutionally embedded in a 'welfare frame' of the help. The other – latent – is more coherent with a well-being frame. Between these two agreements there is a connection but also a contradiction. The explicit contract, with its rules, actions, tools, more close to the professional expertise of 'social worker' and 'expert' is the rational institutional frame of the relationship. But the real content of the relationship is based on an implicit hidden contract with its different rules, actions and tools (more close to counseling). The difference between these two kinds of agreements creates a sort of opacity and ambiguity in the relationship and the difficulty 'to tell to our colleagues the content of our job, what we really do', as a participant to the laboratory told. Some criticism is expressed concerning the fact that the organization and the institution, the companies – and of course the users as well – are unable to understand their 'real job' and see the guidance process in the frame of a match between demand and offer. In this process the counselor needs to 'reaffirm their role', which is the title of the third story in the word of another lifelong guidance practitioner.

Reaffirming the role

> The lady is Italian and belongs to a middle-class family, she has two children and is living in a special situation because she has been dumped by her husband and one of her two children was recently born. I feel that this person has no resource to activate at this time, and has no intention of doing it. She is a very pampered and spoiled person, used to having from others and she does not work. She came because she stopped working soon after getting married in order to devote herself to her house and raising her children and then her husband dumped her. Someone suggested she should visit us. May be she will strive to get things on her own but for now she expects to get them only from the others. At one point she told me I was bossy, because I tried to assert myself. At first she complained about this but, afterwards, she thanked me. I can stimulate you, but if there is no substance.... You, too, guidance counselor, you find it difficult to believe, you feel like a little doll there: having to do your job, you can't send people away. However, before, when you were able to do it, you have made attempts. On those occasions I experienced 'What am I doing, maybe I could devote myself to other people who need me'. Now, for example, she has been telling me for a month that she's not seeking work, she prefers to wait until September when her children go to kindergarten. Anyway she came, she allowed me to make some entries in the application forms but no avail...and you can't say no. It took me a month before I told her I'd see her in September. She is a person who needs to talk, she doesn't need a job, but a confessor. I find myself facing a closure, she is a person who is ill. Since I am a public servant, by definition, I have to offer a public service. Some situations...I cannot close them in the bud avoiding wasting them. You know that a person lacks the autonomy, but requires you to do something, what do

you say? She arrives with a request related to the service. And you put her curriculum on the website:

During the discussion someone said: 'The role of guidance counseling practitioner appears to be an ongoing role and everyone sees it differently. It is necessary to reformulate it every time. Although your role should be clear, it is asserted many times, in different ways'. And another participant said: 'You should find a way for which the person uses the service, but autonomously. Maybe she must collide with reality. It is not enough for someone just to tell her'.

The role of an official offering resources such as information can in some way be standardized and organized through routines. Their job is inside a frame aiming to reduce the ambiguity: the success is the optimization of the match reducing the ambiguities and the uncertainty with the help of professional tools. Conversely, the role of guidance counselor or coach concerns helping people to become conscious of their real capabilities and strategies and supporting them in order to make the right choices. In this case the object of the service is less in the 'problem solving' and the success is embedded in the reframing process itself.

3. Some suggestions

From these and other stories and discussions, some suggestions come out to support the shift to a new appreciative role of guidance practitioners that matches with the concept of capability:

(1) The unexpected can be a mark of success and can be welcomed. In an appreciative perspective it is relevant not only because it allows practitioners to learn from their practice, but also because it means the expression of the otherness and of the uniqueness of the helped person and of her real capabilities.

(2) Because of the relevance and of positivity of the unexpected, it is very important that the feedback process should be an integrant part of the agreement from the beginning. The feedback must be detected both during the relationship and after the closure of the relationship. Feedback means listening, paying attention and learning.

(3) In order to help people to express their real freedom and capabilities, a balance between action and inertia is needed. It means to give people room to express their voice reacting and facilitating their reaction in an appreciative way. All this means professional autonomy, professional stand, ability to keep 'the right distance', as well as a strong listening competence and an empathetic emotional support.

(4) The meaning of autonomy can also be seen as a 'space of appreciative interaction' or 'space for the feedback'. That means physical space, time, relationship management and some 'power' on this space of facilitation inside the organization (almost a clear recognition).

(5) At the same time, in order to avoid to be taken up by the strategies of the clients and users, the guidance counseling practitioners need to strengthen their professional network and increase the professional support by their working group. 'The working group helps to maintain objectivity, it takes you back to reality, so you can reprocess the dynamics of 'do not know what happened and I do not know how to move'.

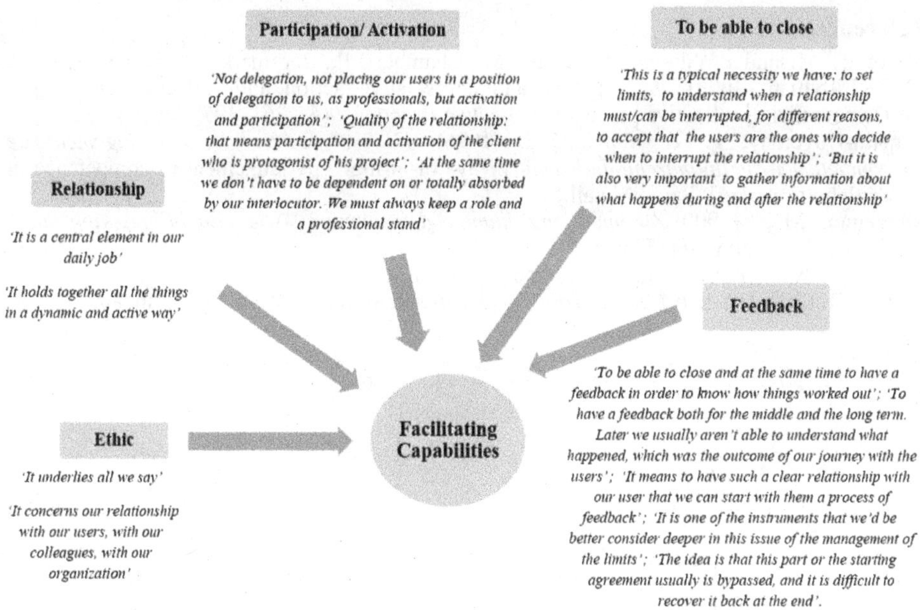

Figure 1. Facilitating capabilities through reflection.

(6) The meaning of point (5) is that the role of the group cooperation is not only that of giving professional support and overcoming the isolation. It also has to do with supporting reflective learning of the individuals through the reflective learning of the group as well. The PAAR methodology is supportive of this necessity.

In a brainstorming meeting in one laboratory, COL practitioners were asked to write on to 'Post-Its' of different colors, from one to five, key words related to the three fields, 'personnel development/individual', 'I as professional and my organization' and 'the relations with my clients'. Then the 'Post-It' of the same colors were clustered in order to focus the most relevant thematic issues inside each field and a key word was chosen as a tag for each cluster. Finally, a narrative was proposed to clarify and focus the meaning of each cluster, the process underlying its identification, the connection with the other clusters. In Figure 1 I propose the clusters and some excerpts from the related narratives concerning the field 'the relations with my clients'. The key phrase of the title of this paper, 'facilitating capabilities' gives an interesting focus to all the clusters.

References

Ghaye, T., Melander-Wikman, A., Kisare, M., Chambers, P., Bergmark, U., Kostenius, C., & S. Lillyman (2008). Participatory and appreciative action and reflection (PAAR) – Democratizing reflective practices. *Reflective Practice, 9*(4), 361–397.

Eymard-Duvernay, F., & Marchal, E. (1996). *Façons de recruter: Le jugement de compétemce sur le marché de travail* [Ways of hiring: The judgement of competence in the labour market]. Paris: Métailié.

Nussbaum, M.C. (2000). *Women and human development: The capabilities approach.* Cambridge: Cambridge University Press.

Sen, A. (2009). *The idea of justice.* London: Penguin.

Sennett, R. (2003). *Respect in a word of inequality.* New York: Norton and Company.

Empowering people through reframing: experiences of guidance practitioners in a public network of career centres

Massimo Tomassini[a], Antonella Barile[b], Eleonora Fiumara[b] and Paola Scarpello[b]

[a]*University of Roma Tre, Rome, Italy;* [b]*Work Guidance Centres, Municipality of Rome, Italy*

In this article, *empowerment* is assumed as a phenomenon strictly related to *agency* dynamics and to the reflective abilities of actors in a given organisational context, which allow their own personal and professional fulfilment. The article is the outcome of a reflective interview in which the authors involved themselves, at the end of a two-year co-operation for the development of the Leonardo da Vinci Reflect-OR project. Five main processes of empowerment are taken into account related to the paths of professional identity construction, the opportunities for competence development, the functioning of the community of practice, the spaces for emotions and the opportunities for transformation. In the final remarks, the subjective side of empowerment is emphasised and some lines for future deepening of the above issues are highlighted.

1. Questions about empowerment

The concept of *empowerment* played a central role in the Reflect-OR project as it was a project aimed at implementing a broad-scope methodology for practitioners' development in career guidance public services. Written at the end of this two-year project, this article tries to provide a number of considerations about empowerment, drawing upon the direct perceptions and interpretations of the authors, all engaged in implementing Reflect-OR[1] in one of the project's contexts: the network of Centres for Career Guidance (*Centri per l'Orientamento al Lavoro*) (COLs) of the Municipality of Rome. The article has been produced through a reflective interview in which three of the COLs workers, stimulated by a researcher/facilitator, engaged in the projects since its very first design phases, tried to shed some light on the real nature of empowerment.

What does empowerment mean, in the very end? Which are the implications of this evocative, but also ambiguous and sometimes abused, term? Which way the contradiction between an idea that is intrinsically related to the acquisition of 'power', on one side and, on the other side, the work and organisation realities in which such an acquisition faces structural obstacles and hinders? What does it mean to introduce a participative and appreciative methodology in a contradictory organisational context in which empowerment did not represent a shared value until recently?

The following sections address such questions. In sections 2 and 3, a short theoretical framework and a depiction of some reflective interview characteristics are respectively provided. In sections 4 to 8, some of the outcomes of the reflective interview are presented (in a way necessarily compressed because of the nature and space of this contribution).[2] In section 9 the reader will find brief final remarks related to the Reflect-OR experience together with suggestions for future action-reflection interventions aimed at enhancing the empowerment opportunities of people living and working in different contexts.

2. Empowerment: some preliminary remarks

In general, *empowerment* refers to individual opportunities in terms of 'power, choice and responsibility' originated by specific kinds of power re-distribution in the work place (Haar, 2006). However, a rather marked hiatus can be identified between top-down and bottom-up views regarding the nature of such a re-distribution. In top-down perspectives, typical of functionalistic approaches, the re-distribution is considered as an outcome of specific management strategies and, as a consequence, empowerment is assumed as an instrument for the delegation of decision-making and management responsibilities towards lower-level employees (Mills, 2006).

On the other hand, within the more bottom-up perspectives, different views coexist. Those who underline the emergence of new organisational forms (lean, network, information-based, heterarchical, and many more) usually consider 'top' and 'down' as increasingly meaningless references and think that the re-distribution of decisions and tasks – and power as a consequence – is an unavoidable step for the search of organisational effectiveness. Such re-distribution effects are taken into account by innumerable authors who emphasise the rise of new professionalism and the knowledge-based nature of the majority of occupations in modern economies. Under a different viewpoint, the growing opportunities for non-traditional power equilibria are pointed out by post-modern approaches, which consider the force relations among individuals and social groups as the core issue of their analyses, but also tend to show how these are structured in relation to local and unstable substrates, highly variable from case to case. From a different perspective, 'critical' views about managerial ideologies depict current empowerment-based approaches in human resource management as deceitful and manipulative (Bauman, 2008). Even the bottom-up perspective as such, from this viewpoint, is deemed to be a different way of establishing inner conditionings in relation to management imperatives for order and productivity (Marzano, 2008).

In this article a *middle-down-up* notion of empowerment is retained. Such a definition is related to an idea of empowerment as an outcome of specific configurations of the *agency/structure* relationship in specific contexts. Following Giddens (1979), *structure* can be seen as the set of rules and resources that, in given context, facilitates or hinders social action. Such rules and resources are incorporated in recurrent social practices, but at the same time are autonomous from them. *Structure* cannot be identified with *organisation*. It represents an entity that is objective, enduring and external to the social actors. *Agency*, on the other side, is a 'flow of intentional actions', reflexively regulated, exposed to unconscious effects and unintended outcomes. It becomes in some way visible insofar as actors produce narrations and justifications (*accounts*) of their own actions. Agency, as an emerging correlate of structure, is based on the individuals' power of contrasting the structure's pressures and of adjusting structural rules and resources for their own advantage.

Arguably, *reflective empowerment* is a self-enabling phenomenon, strictly related to *agency*, through which those living in a given work and organisational context may build, over time, their own opportunities for personal and professional fulfilment (see Figure 1). The core causes of empowerment are seen as closely linked to reflective/reflexive abilities of understanding, choice and action which can accrue the actors' subjective potentialities and can foster the material, relational and emotional advantages stemming from the participation in a specific action context.

An overall analysis of the Reflect-OR project activities and outcomes (see also the other articles of this special issue) enabled us to articulate the above vision of empowerment into five main processes:

- the paths of professional identity construction (which ways actors reflect on their personal and professional being, and to what extent such reflection helps them in reshaping their professional lives);
- the opportunities for competence development (to what extent competence is individually and collectively recognised and rewarded);
- the functioning of the community of practice (to what extent work practices constitute the 'situated' ground for goals identification, mutual learning and cultural artefacts);
- the spaces for emotions (to what extent emotions are recognised and considered as action triggers); and
- the opportunities for transformation (to what extent innovation is possible through the re-framing of shared visions and the emergence of new action paradigms).

The reflective interview (see note 2) was devoted to exploring such processes. The ideas emerged in relation to each of them are reported in the following sections,[3] after a brief introduction about the context.

3. The intervention's context

The COL network is composed of 16 units. Historically, it has been created not through a specific strategic choice and a subsequent organisational setup, but as an

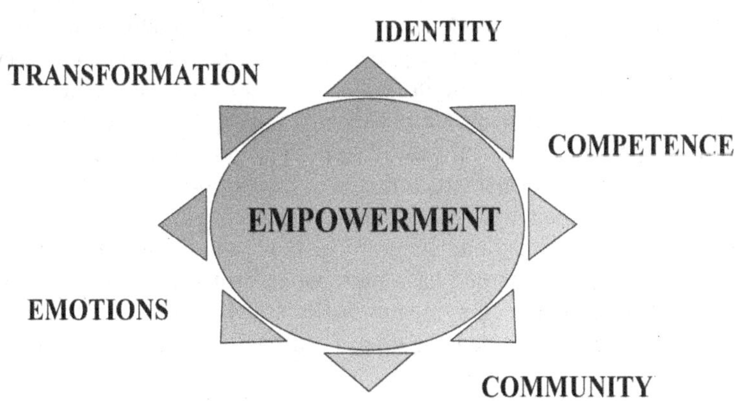

Figure 1. Five processes of reflective empowerment.

aggregation process involving already existing autonomous small guidance organisations (belonging to the third sector, or linked to the trade unions or constituted as social co-operatives). In a period of about fifteen years, starting from 1990, the Municipality of Rome has promoted the aggregation of them through different measures (including a project for guidance services' development funded by the European Social Fund). In 2005, all employees of these services were hired by the municipality, and the COL network officially started its activities. Each single COL developed its own activities, having as reference both general institutional objectives (guidance activities, mainly for disadvantaged target groups) and project-related objectives linked to local social demands and to temporary agreements with other organisations (e.g., schools, vocational education and training (VET) centres, associations, research institutions, etc.).

COLs are small-sized organisations. Their average staff is not above the six people dealing with two main kinds of activities:

(1) reception and information for people willing to explore their own labour market opportunities; and
(2) consulting support for those having subjective difficulties in work and learning paths, and needing help in relation to them.

Some boundaries are established between these two main activities, to be performed in a sequence (reception comes necessarily before counselling), and in fact assigned to different levels of personnel (reception is usually carried out either by lower-level workers or by students on internships.[4] However, these boundaries are not rigid, at least in one sense. Those employees welcoming the public do not consult while, on the other side, consultants also play information and assistance roles and a number of other ones as well (even together with the 'receptionists'). In organisational terms, what is currently defined as the COLs 'network' is in fact an organisational structure articulated into a 'centre' (the XIV Municipality's Department) and a number of 'peripheries': the 17 COLs, each one with its own specific traits.

Considering that single COLs are components of a scattered and fragmented network, the average level of inter-organisational communication and sense-making among them is considered not too bad by workers, although several problems persist due to local differences in dealing with day-to-day activities and in interpreting the organisational mission. The network is not yet really established but the way is open towards such a goal. On the contrary, the centre/periphery relations are mostly of a formal-bureaucratic nature. The centre generates very limited strategic inputs and, so far, has intended its own role to be in terms of control of performances' regularity (opening hours, work attendances, etc.). This is a consequence of the missed accomplishment of the original organisational design and strategy. In the first half of the 2000s, in parallel with the formal structuring process, important changes took place in the management team. The municipality management team that initially supported the COLs' creation was disbanded and its political momentum subsided. Moreover, an institutional contradiction emerged as a national reform process established a new network of local placement centres institutionally attached to provinces, also having guidance functions. Therefore the COLs had to further clarify their own mission and *raison-d'être.*

As a whole, following an agency/structure interpretative framework, the formal organisation that structurally embodies *rules and resources* for COLs' functioning is still in search of a clear self-definition and is kept together by formal bureaucratic criteria within a survival perspective. At the same time, in the largest majority of COLs, an *agency* push from individuals and small groups is manifest towards self-development, based on local resources and abilities and focused on social reference interests. Such agency tends to counter the bureaucratic tendencies and to recover initiative and empowerment spaces on the basis of direct link with local social needs and of commonalities and alliances with other institutions (schools, VET centres, social assistance centres and many more). Due to the interplay of such factors, the 'centre' has tended to take an objectively dis-empowering function over time, while, in parallel, in a different COL a significant need for role confirmation and action empowerment has tended to grow up and to find ways for affirmation.

4. Professional identity

The agency/structure perspective helps in underlining the central role of the professional identity dimension. For COLs workers, far from being stable and once-for-all established, the latter appears as a continuously re-built entity, showing strong links with the individuals' reflexively constituted *self-identity* on one side (Giddens, 1992) and the dynamics of work practices on the other side. Such traits are evidently reinforced in the Italian reality. Guidance activities carried out in COLs have much to do with purposes of *lifelong learning career counselling* (LLCG), according to a definition currently in use in scientific literature and in European guidelines.[5] However, as in the overall Italian context, guidance is still an insufficiently recognised function both in social and legal terms, LLCG cannot be referred to a clearly defined set of procedures and behaviours. On the contrary, it is continuously enmeshed with information, assistance and other functions of this kind. In COLs' work organisation there are boundaries between information and consultation activities, but the professional role and even the job title (*orientatore*) can be indifferently applied to workers performing both simpler information roles and more complex consultation roles.

Given such a background, those more involved in career counselling accept the multifaceted and even ambiguous nature of their activity, and are engaged in bottom-up enforcement of it because of the resulting greater satisfaction and clearer social acknowledgment. In many ways their professional identity is of an 'emerging' nature, in which different action models converge, taken from other professions (in particular, but not only, the counselling and psychotherapeutic professions), and is adapted in relation to mixed and ever changing needs:[6]

> Our work is a puzzle composed of different pieces to be put together. The aim is not reaching a pre-defined shape but getting to a construction which might allow the reproduction of identity and motivation for us. Our work is made significant by our practices as such, by what we do day-by-day. For instance, yesterday, during a support activity for migrants in which I had a pivotal role, I realised how important is our facilitation function regarding people having cultural and linguistic difficulties. Facilitation is a further piece of my game: I must be aware of it, although one cannot find any recognition of it.

> I developed my identity in the world of guidance starting from a psychology background. Over time I got a passion for this world. Now, after 17 years, I feel that the process is accomplished: I perceive myself as an *orientatrice*, and my entourage do so as well,

> while for a long time they considered me as a psychologist. There is a lot to do in this context. We have to bring our help in many different situations. And this requires that we really play this game and are able to re-invent us continuously.

> Our bosses think about us as clerks, not as professionals. They do not care very much about the ways in which we cope with our challenges and produce concrete results. This is a dis-empowering factor for us. But our work cannot be done without engagement and will for change. We tend to continuously improve our performances: we are developing approaches that work. We are finding ways for showing it: Reflect-OR is one of them.

5. Competence

Being *empowered* largely means to be able to shape one's own professional competence, which, in turn, depends on reflection about both one's experience and intentions for change. Individuals and groups have simultaneously to express their engagement, will and power in order to develop well-being and satisfaction in their work contexts (Ghaye, 2001). This competence/empowerment process also appears, besides the one related to professional identity, as highly contingent in COL workers' experience:

> Our identity and competences are linked to 'listening' capabilities typical of counselling techniques, but evolve according to specific practical needs as they require tailor-made solutions. I realised that most of what I do comes from similarity and approximation. The essence of 'competence' for me is the ability to introduce continuous shifts in my action repertoire, implementing what has to be used in a specific situation and not implementing what is inappropriate.

> Competence means versatility for me. I deal with persons who are very different from one another. I must be able to treat a teenager getting inside his insecurities, his unwillingness neither of studying nor of working, his absolute distance from the world. And, in the next hour, I have somebody aged between 50 and 60 in front of me, somebody who is going to miss his job: I must be able to deal with his despair and fear. In the two cases I must be different, and I think my competence is nested in such difference.

6. Community of practice

In the *practice* dimension, different aspects converge in the material side of activities that are daily carried out: the sense-making about what is going on and what is to be done, the ways in which the capabilities have to be implemented and the forms that internal and external relations have to take. The *community* perspective helps in understanding the ways in which such aspects are continuously negotiated and identity and competence continuously reproduced. In the COL network, considering its genesis and internal dynamics, things are more complex than in some other organisations. Every worker is in fact at the same time member of two communities: the micro-organisational one and the 'network' one:

> Our activity is composed by many elements: we give information, we listen to problems, we do guidance counselling through specific tools (like 'competence budgets' for instance). In some cases our relation with the client lasts the time of a short meeting, in other cases a longer and more dense kind of activity is needed. The openness of our mission gives rise to different inconveniences: sometimes we risk to go beyond our assigned role with difficult persons whose needs are far beyond the 'job' as such. What

> do we have to do? Up to which point do we have to reach? This is a relevant example of a permanent questioning within our group. But this is also an example of how it is difficult the tuning with the rest of the network. What do the others do? Which are their real practices? Which is the 'community' for me?
>
> I tend to realise that the 'network' is in some way a recent phenomenon and that its community effects are emerging only in the last periods. I have been working here for 10 years but I had the chance of meeting colleagues of the other COLs only four years ago in a training course. In this course we got to know each other and generated common tools and procedures. It was a good starting point. Now there are much more relationships but we still have to construct a real network.

The network and the extended community are mostly growing up through the participation in external projects:

> Reflect-OR is an excellent example of the ways in which a viable community should be built up, through reciprocal recognition and the creation of common goals. There are other examples (another European project with French partners; some projects developed with schools and VET centres; a research study on juvenile deviant behaviours which implied the participation of several COLs in co-operation with the University of Rome).
>
> All these activities have generated something that might be better labelled in terms of 'community of motivation', in which we recognise each other not only as bearers of common interests but also as persons and professionals characterised by specific modes of being and acting.

7. Emotions

In a context such as the one of COLs, relevant empowerment phenomena can be understood when one overcomes the traditional dimensions of organisational analysis, only focused on the socio-cognitive aspects of working and relational practices. The emotional dimension of work and organisation must also be carefully taken into account, due to at least two different reasons:

(1) a larger consideration of emotions in a mostly female work environment and culture (as the COLs network is); and
(2) the familiarity with emotions as integral component of a working life exposed to a difficult audience and, in some way, as a current 'working tool' for guidance counselling activities.

Living and working in such an environment naturally implies the development of some levels of 'emotional awareness' (Dalai Lama & Ekman, 2008) having specific physical/mental manifestations, and of 'emotional intelligence': self-perceived ability of recognising own and others' feelings and of positively handling emotions at the personal and relational level (Goleman, 1995):

> Recently, in order to implement what was established by an agreement with the provincial employment offices, we had to deal with a number of cases of over-50s who already lost their jobs or are very close to be unemployed. I feel the effect of my own professional empowerment in talking with these people: I'm increasingly more able to overcome negative emotions and to put positive empathy into action. The parallel listening to ourselves and to the client is a fundamental component of our work: this helps me in keeping in touch with my inner reactions and to avoid frustrating and depressive

> attitudes. I have to also take care of myself, in particular when I'm kept by thoughts such as 'I cannot do anything useful in such a desperately hopeless case'; 'I have no answer to provide'; 'what am I doing here'. If I understand my emotional background I'm more able to cope the situations that generate such thoughts.

Two important phenomena have to be underlined regarding the emotional dimension. On the one hand, COLs actors appear as active reflective observers of their own emotions. On the other hand, such levels of reflection have significant effects on organisational action and on forms of self-empowerment that are largely based on ethical presuppositions. As put forward within the *organising reflection* approach, by bringing to the fore the emotions that are part of the dynamic flow of interacting between social and political forces, important organising processes emerge that underpin the way individuals make sense of their own experiences (Antonacopoulou, 2004):

> When we get to emotionally intense points, our sense of the team gets also reinforced. Recently, for instance, when we had to deal with the over-50s, we had a double reaction. We reinforced the levels of our mutual help but we also found new practical courses of action while discussing our emotional states. For example, we considered it wiser to 'go out', to do something that we never did before in these terms: we directly contacted both the small businesses that were putting in jeopardy our clients' employment with them and the public bodies having a say on these issues. We went beyond the classical lifelong career guidance action framework and tried to establish new action patterns. Of course this cannot be a constant modus operandi: we are not equipped for doing it systematically. And nevertheless it was important for us. Afterwards we reflected on such a behaviour and realised that emotions can be the trigger even of mobilising (not paralysing) effects.

8. Transformation

All the above processes, each one with its specificities, tend in many ways towards transformations of the present situation. People empowerment, from this viewpoint, is concurrent with social-cultural-organisational transformations. For COLs workers, being empowered means being positively involved in circuits of emerging transformations based on step-by-step re-framing of action reality. Such re-framing should be seen both as a cognitive endeavour (Mezirow & Taylor, 2009) and as the result of different processes' interplay in which social, emotional and ethical factors are also involved (Ghaye et al., 2008) and qualitatively characterise the overall transformation. The Reflect-OR project played a significant role in such transformative empowerment:

> The project gave us chances for expressing fears, emotions, difficult moments within a totally new for us (appreciative) approach. The presence of external facilitators was in fact of great support. They provided innovative keys which helped us in putting some aspects of our collective discourse back in their own perspective. For example, we are now able to better see the negative effects of the contraposition 'we/them' between us and the department's managers. We overcame the 'wall-against-wall' perception of this relationship.

> At the beginning it was difficult to identify the 'success stories' concerning our macro-organisation. However, when we were able to do it, we perceived us as having made important steps forward. Now it is as if we were more aware of our reality and, because of it, less afraid of our manager. Our propensities towards conflict are now better channelled. We can understand even 'their' problems, as having deep roots in the structures

of administrative action in our context, where it is impossible to escape from formal procedures. While we are even less prone confuse our role image with that of the 'clerk', at the same time we are increasingly aware of the need of behaving according to formal procedures.

I must admit that in the past I was somehow disgusted by the world of procedures. When our managers were asking us to follow the bureaucratic procedures I tended to refuse to listen to them. Now I realise that we should take possession of these instruments in order to use them appropriately in relation to our ends. For better or worse they are a component of our world: this kind of understanding makes me feel more mature and responsible, more empowered regarding my activity and my position in the organisation.

9. Concluding remarks

The reflective interview presented in this article has been a positive experience for us. It has proved to be a valuable means for the re-exploration of our individual and group experiences. Far from being aimed at merely eliciting contents from field actors – like traditional *distal* research tools do – this kind of collective exercise functioned as a *proximal* trigger for us, fostering subjective awareness and shared understanding processes. It showed interesting opportunities for even bringing about some research advances. In many ways, the use and results of the reflective interview seem to represent a small but not insignificant contribution to closing – as envisaged in recent organisation research – the chasm between practice-driven theorising of what people do in their workplace and the academic theory-driven theorising about it (Yanow, 2006, quoted in Nicolini, 2009).

We can think about empowerment as a phenomenon largely dependent on individual and collective interpretative efforts, or, in other terms, as the outcome of accounts that hinge on closer understandings of *structure* dynamics and that tend to step-by-step reshape their own local *agency*. Following the terms briefly introduced in section 2, the COLs seem to represent an interesting case of 'prevalence of agency on structure'. Even in that contradictory organisation, constantly at risk of being blocked by social and organisational factors, the workers show specific abilities for the identification of *affordances* (i.e., the real 'possibilities for action') present in their own contexts and for the exploitation of them. The main trigger of such emerging and continuously evolving abilities is a general need of 'being themselves', i.e., being recognised, valorised, acknowledged in relation to – and on the basis of – their activities and results.

The self-valorisation of *subjective* attitudes and dispositions at the individual and at the small group level represents the crucial underpinning of these abilities. In the COLs' case, it is particularly evident that empowering processes are not only related to local historical-contextual conditions but also to autonomously settled values and aspirations. The interpretations that we provided about our own empowerment dynamics largely appeared as stemming from personal stories and work-based learning paths. Reflectivity (regarding reality) and reflexivity (regarding the perceived subjective position in the reality) – one can conclude – are not at all an automatic outcome of experience. They require specific dispositions that can of course be favoured by a certain kind of contextual structural arrangements but are basically rooted in individual abilities to let them coherently grow. In this process even the individuals' 'ultimate concerns' about personal projects play an important role. Together with the idea of empowerment as a social construction, the reflective interview seems in fact to bring about the idea of empowerment as maintained by the continuous interplay of individual 'internal conversations' (Archer, 2003) each one regarding the directions to follow in order to satisfy important personal concerns. In this sense the hypotheses that provided the overall framework of our interview (such as those about, for instance, the self-identity or the emotional side of work) should be integrated by a further – and in many ways different – view that assumes as crucial the role of reflexivity, manifested through the 'internal conversation', in an intermediate position between agency and structure (Archer, 2007).

The participative appreciative action and reflection (PAAR) methodology has positively stimulated our reflection about empowerment processes, providing conceptual, relational and rhetoric artefacts that helped shed light on the continuum between the individual, small group and overall collective/organisational dimensions. These artefacts allowed us to review our practices, putting the focus alternatively on details (such as in small stories with clients) and on the wider action landscape within bureaucratic organisations. This process has something to do with the 'zooming-in/zooming-out' image recently suggested in order to define the navigation through work practices using both different investigation methods and theoretical lenses (Nicolini, 2009). In terms of empowerment, such focus switching helped our self-understanding and paved the way for positive evolutions of the guidance practitioner's role, of the functioning of practitioners' communities and the of the relational policies within a public administration.

Future implementations of the Reflect-OR methodology should capitalise on its multi-level potential, trying to deepen the interplay between action and reflection at the crossing of the 'first person' level (the personal/professional *I*), of the 'second person' level (the *I-you* and *I-we* of the community) and of the 'third person' level (the *we-they* of overall organisation). The success of future implementations will very much depend on the capacity of supporting a shift from a *language of certainty* to a *language of inquiry* (Yanow, 2009), as Reflect-OR in COLs did. Also, in other contexts it may be possible to harvest the fruits of such a shift — and those of the *passionate humility,* which usually underpins the language of inquiry (Yanow, 2009) – as happened in the COLs' case where we put ourselves under discussion and found new ways of empowerment through a kind of reframing in which we tried to alternate appreciation and sincerity. Some of the possibilities are shown in Figure 2.

Notes

1. This article has been prepared by a group of Reflect-OR participants who met several times specifically for this purpose. Antonella Barile, Eleonora Fiumara and Paola Scarpello – guidance counselling practitioners – work in the *Centri di Orientamento al Lavoro* (COLs) of the Municipality of Rome. They took part in the project's steering task force. Massimo Tomassini – researcher, counsellor, contract professor at the University of Roma Tre – played different roles in project's design, co-ordination, facilitation and research.
2. 'Reflective interview' is the definition attributed to the activity that this article is based on. It consisted of three sessions (of about three hours each) aimed at going through the Reflect-OR contents and results with the help of an interpretative self-questioning grid concerning five processes of empowerment (see above). The grid was previously created by the researcher-facilitator on the basis of his experience of the whole Reflect-OR project activities (mostly consisting in storytelling by COLs workers within 'reflective workshops'). The sessions took a form close to the one of an open focus-group, through which the three authors, having an operational role, were allowed to re-think their own overall

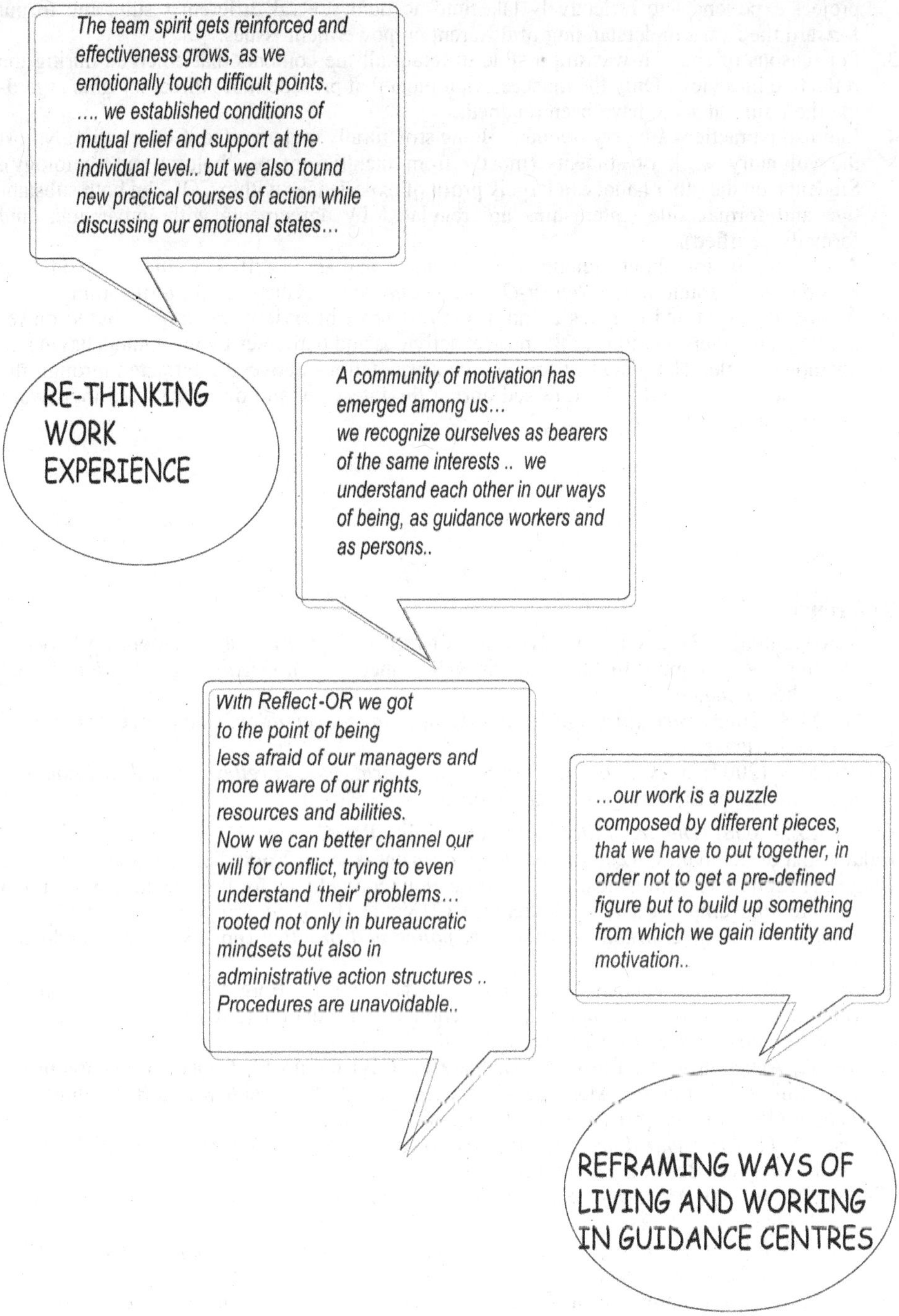

Figure 2. Some possibilities for action.

project experience, to reflectively take into account several different results and to put forward their own understanding of different empowerment issues.

3. For reasons of space it was impossible to retain all the contents that emerged during the reflective interview. Only the most relevant dicta that provide more direct insights regarding the issues at stake have been retained.
4. Internship practices are very frequent. Being structurally understaffed, COLs willingly host the voluntary work of students (mostly from faculties of psychology and sociology). Students, on the other hand, can largely profit of experiences within COLs on both substantive and formal side (internships are regulated by agreements with universities and formally certified).
5. A short discussion about lifelong career guidance and about different guidance models in Europe can be found in the *Reflect-OR project fieldbook* (Ghaye et al., forthcoming).
6. As already explained in notes 2 and 3, the reflective interview was largely based on rethinking and interpretations of the project activities and outcomes by the authors having an operational role. The pieces of text shown as quotations above are extracted through the reflections of such authors expressed during the interview and directly regard their work experience in COLs contexts.

References

Antonacopoulou, E.P. (2004). The dynamics of reflexive practice: the relationship between learning and changing. In M. Reynolds & R. Vince (Eds.), *Organising reflection,* 47–64 Aldershot: Ashgate.

Archer, M.S. (2003). *Structure, agency and the internal conversation.* Cambridge: Cambridge University Press.

Archer, M.S. (2007). *Making our way through the world: human reflexivity and social mobility.* Cambridge: Cambridge University Press.

Bauman, Z. (2008). *The art of life.* Cambridge: Polity Press.

Dalai Lama & Eckman, P. (2008). *Emotional awareness.* New York: Times Books.

Ghaye, T. (2001). Empowerment through reflection: competence for the new millennium or a case for the emperor's new clothes? In C. Velde (Ed.), *International perspectives on competence in the workplace: Research, policy and practice* (pp. 181–220). Dordrecht: Kluver.

Ghaye, T., Melander Wickman A., Kisare M., Chambers P., Bergmark U., & Lillyman S. (2008). Participatory and appreciative action and reflection (PAAR) – Democratising reflective practices. *Reflective Practice, 9*, 4.

Ghaye, T., Alexandrov A., Barile A., Bednarz F., Cavicchiolo E., Consoli F., Giannini D., Lucattini B., Marchi S., Markova G., Sarcina R., & Tomassini M. (forthcoming) *The Reflect-OR fieldbook* [provisional title], Roma: Giunti.

Giddens, A. (1979). *Central problems in social theory. Action, structure and contradiction in Social analysis.* Berkley: UCLA Press.

Giddens, A. (1991). *Modernity and self-identity. Self and society in the late modern age,* Cambridge: Polity Press.

Goleman, P. (1995). *Emotional intelligence: what it is and why it can matter more that IQ.* New York: Bantam Books.

Haar, J.M. (2006). Empowerment. *Encyclopedia of Educational Leadership and Administration.* Thousand Oaks: SAGE.

Marzano, M., (2009). *Estensione del dominio della manipolazione: dall'azienda alla vita privata.* Milan: Mondadori.

Mezirow J., & Taylor E., (2009). *Transformative learning in practice: Insights from community, workplace, and higher education.* San Francisco: Jossey-Bass.

Mills, P.K. (2006). Empowerment. *Encyclopedia of Career Development.* Thousand Oaks: Sage.

Nicolini, D. (2009). Zooming in and out: Studying practices by switching theoretical lenses and trailing connections. *Organisation Studies 30*(12), 1391–1418.

Yanow, D. (2006). Talking about practices: on Julian Orr's talking about machines. *Organisation Studies, 27*(12), 1743–1756.

Yanow, D., (2009). Ways of knowing. Passionate humility and reflective practice in research and management. *The American Review of Public Administration, 36*(6), 579–601.

Reflective practice, appreciative regard and organizational wellbeing: an experience in Swiss employment services

Furio Bednarz[a], Elisa Cavicchiolo[b], Simona Marchi[b] and Massimo Tomassini[c]

[a]ECAP Foundation, Lugano, Switzerland; [b]Department of Economics, 'Sapienza' University of Rome, Rome, Italy and Reflective Learning Italy, Rome, Italy; [c]University of Roma Tre, Rome, Italy

The article presents experiences and lessons learned in the framework of a participative appreciative action and reflection (PAAR) laboratory organized in Ticino (Switzerland) by the ECAP Foundation, testing methods and tools developed by the Reflect-OR project. PAAR potentialities and pre-requisites are evaluated in a specific organizational context, provided by a public-private partnership in the field of active labor market policies. Coaching jobseekers, according to principles of empowerment and self-direction, is the task of private service providers; they work on behalf of public employment services, aiming at fostering activation and social responsibility of the 'clients'. Clients are in fact asked to activate themselves for a quick reintegration in the job market, in order to reduce costs due to welfare indemnities. Well-established rules, reducing the autonomy of professionals and their organization, inform the partnership, producing sometimes tensions and misunderstandings. The article draws on representations and codes affecting the relationships between coaches, clients, mandatory institutions and service providers, detecting how and to which extent reflective practices and tools could be valued to improve the overall quality of the partnership. We focus on appreciative regard and story telling as means to improve awareness and competences of the actors, enabling personal and organizational learning processes.

The laboratory

A Swiss laboratory organized the framework of the Reflect-OR project, involving a dozen of trainers and counselors active in ECAP Ticino – UNIA training center. They belong to a wider task force, in charge of supporting jobseekers, working according to a mandate given to ECAP by local public employment services (*Ufficio Misure Attive, Sezione del Lavoro del Dipartimento Finanze ed Economia del Cantone Ticino*). The laboratory, managed in cooperation with Reflective Learning Italy (RLI), has been articulated in different directions and activities, along a pathway of collective reflective sessions, moderated by the authors, acting as facilitators. The path, designed on the basis of the experience of the *Centri per l'Orientamento al Lavoro* (COL) laboratory in Rome,[1] was articulated in a phase devoted to context analysis – based on a participative research processes – and in sessions focusing on relational dynamics linking participants to their clients, their colleagues and the organization to which they belong. The discussion in the group, adopting 'story telling' methods, put in practice 'appreciative' techniques, reflections, 'normally' fed by critical incidents (Soini, 2000; Stroobants, Chambers, & Clarke, 2007), that were stimulated by successful experiences, valued as positive triggers for setting and solving organizational blocks and misunderstandings.

In this paper we would like to deal with inputs and lessons learned during more or less 12 months of activity and encounters, which opened new perspectives in the way management and members of ECAP's working group were trying to re-define their relational patterns. From a theoretical point of view, we will refer to concepts and notions clarified by Massimo Tomassini,[2] moving from a *middle-down-up* notion of *empowerment*, even if our paper better focuses more on effects and features of an appreciative regard as a means to promote organizational reflection and transformation than on empowerment effects and trajectories. Nevertheless the *agency/structure* relationship, as defined by Tomassini, according to Giddens, plays a fundamental role also in our specific context, and therefore we should constantly bear it in mind reading results and potentialities of the laboratory.

At the same time, the five main processes of empowerment emerging in Rome's COLs experience can be usefully taken in account to interpret Ticino's laboratory in a comparative perspective. We will focus on efforts made by ECAP's coaches in reshaping their *professional identity*, trying to connect change and new opportunities for *competence* development and recognition. We will try to detect to which extent daily work practices of the group constitute the 'situated' ground for goal identification, mutual learning and the development of a 'community of practice'. We will deal with conflicts and tensions rising up in the group, trying to understand if appreciative regards can contribute to recognition and valuation of *emotions* as positive action triggers. We will conclude our article with some remarks about opportunities and constraints emerging in Ticino (in comparison with Rome's experience) from the point of view of *transformations* induced by PAAR approaches (to what extent innovation is possible through the re-framing of shared visions and the emergence of new action paradigms).

Working for 'their' job: the context

In order to understand achievements and constraints that emerged by applying a PAAR approach, it is necessary to contextualize the dynamics of daily lived experiences by practitioners involved in the laboratory. Since the middle of the 1990s in

Switzerland, passive and active labor market policies (ALMPs) have been managed in an integrated way. Benefits accorded by Unemployment Insurance, on a basis of a general law affecting all salary workers, include both income indemnities and measures helping jobseekers find a new job (training, coaching, temporary work experience etc.). Federal and cantonal authorities are jointly responsible for the governance and implementation of ALMPs; strategies are defined at federal level, but cantons are asked to actually implement them. Cantons normally value private service providers in assuring specialized measures, such as training, guidance and in some cases also professional coaching to support more rapidly and actively jobseekers in their efforts. In Switzerland, as overall in Europe, ALMPs adopted in recent years feature some common choices, summarized by 'employment first' strategies (aiming at preventing long-term unemployment), interlaced with initiatives based on the activation of jobseekers and on risk factors profiling. These choices clearly also inform objectives and roles assigned to private service providers by Swiss public employment services, addressing strategies, methods and to some extent also tools that service providers have to adopt and respect. However, the responsibility of defining action plans and duties of unemployed, including the assignment to specific measures, strictly remains in the hand of public counselors. It means that private organizations and their professionals have a narrow space in which they should move. Clients are normally not motivated, nor free to decide. A huge investment has to be made to welcome clients in order to build a trustful and effective relationship, dealing with clients 'forced' to use coaches' support to avoid monetary and non-monetary sanctions in case of refusal or non participation to the obligatory measure.

Figure 1 gives an overview of measures assigned to jobseekers in Ticino. Actually 72.6% of them belong to the area of so-called 'training and accompaniment measures', including the so-called *Programma di Base* (known under the acronym TRIS (*Tecniche di Ricerca Impiego e Sostegno al collocamento – Job search techniques and support*)) in which ECAP operators involved in the laboratory daily work.

Yearly, the ECAP Foundation is in charge about half of the people assigned to Basic Program measures in Ticino: 1000 unemployed per year. Clients represent a very heterogeneous landscape, considering gender, age and professional profiles. Women are 52% of participants, and they are concentrated in middle and older age cohorts, particularly those witnessing difficulties paid in their job search (such as single parent mothers) and persons trying to enter again the job market after a period of inactivity. At the same time, competition existing at the local level between local workforce and qualified trans-border workers coming from Italy determined a relevant increasing of male unemployment, both young and older people, sometime possessing good qualifications. Jobseekers belong to a wide range of professional profiles, including areas traditionally characterized by mobility and recurrent unemployment (tourism, construction, etc.) and areas particularly affected by restructuring and concurrence affecting even advanced services sectors (such as finance, insurance and ICT).

ECAP coaches operate on the basis of a very structured mandate, engineered by mandatory institution. Mandates define responsibilities, objectives, expected outcomes, sequences, administrative obligations and of course evaluation criteria and indicators to be adopted by external providers. Coaches' activity, and in general private provider's effectiveness, is submitted to a global evaluation, based on articulated criteria and indicators, including:

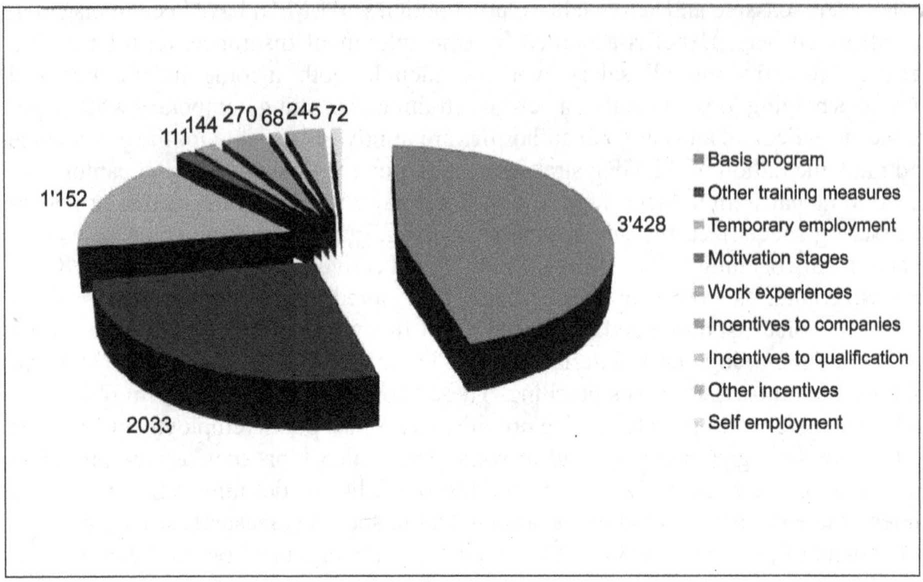

Figure 1. Active labor market policies in Ticino – people involved in different measures (2008). (Source: UMA – Cantone Ticino, 2009).

- perceived quality of information delivered to the clients;
- pedagogical relationship established between coaches and coaches;
- organizational and logistic aspects (resources) of service delivery; and
- sustainability of learning outcomes achieved at the end of the measure, measuring actual development of clients' employability three months after the conclusion, in terms of improved networking, quality of applications and candidature dossiers, autonomy and effectiveness in job search strategies, valuation of supports made available by private providers and of course quantitative results achieved in job search.

A quality system suggests a complex relationship between providers and mandatory institutions; even if it includes also self-evaluation activities, it remains largely based on supervision and evaluative regard of external mandatory institution. Criteria and indicators mainly focus on opinions and behaviors of clients who have to be put in a relationship with the wider legal and socio-economic context affecting job search strategies and realistic achievements. It is easy to understand the influence that these criteria and indicators finally have in orienting both organizations' management choices and the work of the coaches, forcing them to negotiate constantly with different stakeholders: clients providing them with positive and 'sense-making' feed-back, the organization to which they belong (responsible for reaching objectives defined by mandates) and the mandatory institutions in charge of defining strict rules for their action.

Evolving roles and identity construction processes

Ticino's PAAR laboratory took place in a particular period of time that was characterized by an intensive work, due to job losses induced by the global economic crisis.

In 2008 public employment services realized in Ticino over 80,000 individual interviews with jobseekers, assigning over 7500 personal supportive measures (on a stock of about 8000 registered unemployed in the monthly average, and about 20,000 persons who applied for unemployment benefits during the year). At the same time the laboratory accompanied the evolution of coaching and accompaniment logics, shifting from collective activation schemes – allowing counselors to work on group dynamics and deliver proper 'lessons' – to individual one-to-one supportive sessions in which counselors are expected to accelerate the redaction of documents needed to improve candidatures and job search (CV, letters, evidence of skills and competence, etc.), assuring a targeted and individualized accompaniment to the job search, and stimulating autonomy, motivation and responsibility of jobseekers immediately in the initial phase of their unemployment.

Evolving roles demanded ECAP's operators to reinvent and reshape their brand new identity of 'adult trainers' and facilitators, a recognized qualification born in the 1990s. Building a solid professional identity is not an easy task when you deal with a so undetermined 'object' of training, close to guidance, that is helping people define and implement an effective job search strategy. Setting up the laboratory we realized how in the new framework, competence and identity construction processes should have been strictly anchored to self-recognition and *social-organizational* recognition opportunities more than on codified practices. Respect for rules and disposition is not an effective identity trigger, when rules and disposition are a sort of external imposition, not the result of shared codes of behaviors produced by a community of practitioners.

Far apart from their Italian colleagues working in Rome, ECAP's operators are used to move in secure and stable structures. They are expected to follow a well-defined road, from taking in charge clients to providing them with relatively standardized services. A central role in their performance is played by initial and continuing face-to-face interviews, aiming at profiling needs, targeting measures and monitoring the 'agreement' signed between clients and counselors, on expected outcomes of accompaniment and on learning processes integrated in the path. This 'agreement' is at the heart of a delicate trilateral relationship involving clients (jobseekers), coaches and public employment counselors. Coaches are asked to play the role of facilitators, both in some more directive and concrete actions related to the improvement of CVs or candidature dossiers, and training the people in order to enhance their capabilities required to apply for a new job. Coaches are also asked to help participants in recognizing, mapping and valuing their competences, tracing at the end a complete profile of their clients, useful action plans and coherent additional measures. They work according to a very structured plan: phases, tools and outputs are strictly defined on the basis of aims and objectives fixed in the mandate. ECAP is responsible for the fine-tuning of procedures and modalities of the process. The standardization of processes normally facilitates daily activities, provides rules to be followed, helps coaches concentrate on their tasks taking in charge needs and expectations of their clients. However, at the same time it provides limits and constraints to some sensibilities and hampers the valorization of personal styles and approaches to counseling and training, producing some frustration and disappointment.

Changes introduced in the system provoked a destabilization of ECAP's operators' professional identity, shifting its 'locus' from respecting a well-engineered collective path, acting as facilitators in a typical adult training setting, to defining a trustful individual relationship with their clients based on counseling methods and principles. At

Figure 2. Participants at Lugano's laboratory.

the same time this needed to be conditioned by rules and externally driven expectations. This shifting clearly represented a hard challenge, but also a great opportunity for most of Laboratory participants, bringing them to think about their identity in a totally different way. The relational nature of competencies associated to counseling from one side, and the need of situating learning processes (Illeris, 2007; Lave & Wenger, 1991) in a shared context came to the fore.

Context analysis performed during the first sessions of the laboratory put in evidence the delicate balance, made of invisible and 'not written' rules, interlacing the need of respecting general and operational aims defined by mandatory institutions and the attitude of the coaches in managing day-by-day their relational 'obligations', mainly focusing on clients' satisfaction and wellbeing. Positive feedback from clients has the clear effect of empowering the coaches, giving sense to work otherwise affected by a certain anonymity, controlling functions and bureaucratic dispositions, imposed by mandatory institutions via the organization to which they belong. Forced to re-think their professional identity, ECAP's collaborators realized that their competencies were embedded in the way they manage complex relational dynamics, more than in codified practices or existing qualifications. This unexpected discovery influenced their representations about professional roles they are asked to play as well as their expectations. It opened the road to new transitional perspectives that should be interpreted under the lens of tensions characterizing *structure/agency* dynamics in that specific context.

Voice, awareness, responsible action

ECAP's laboratory can be interpreted, from this point of view, as a progressive, even if uncertain and not definite, path from confused organizational disease to responsible and positive collective action. 'Voice' attitudes and individual disappointment characterized the initial stage of the Laboratory, in which an 'I and them' approach could be easily traced. Competence and identity building processes are perceived in an individual perspective. I am acting as an individual player, building temporary alliances with some colleagues, fighting 'for the benefit of the clients' against obstacles provided by organizational constraints and lack of understanding. Dialectics between organization and mandatory institutions were far from being critically evaluated, they were possibly 'judged': delays and uncertainties in giving responses to recognition expectations or in developing new projects promoted by the team are defined as examples of 'cowardly' or 'total sluggishness'.

Problem-solving methods and tools enabled and facilitated the path towards awareness. Awareness means being capable of critical thinking and transformative learning (Mezirow, 2000); of *reflexivity* about both experience and intentions for change:

> What really surprised me was the 'problem solving' methodology, it helps us detect where are problems, when we are blocked on the 'other vision'.

Appreciative inquiry represented the key to change lenses through which reality used to be interpreted:

> We tried to explore the problem, taking in account different points of view; we should me more open minded with our company, are we really sure that we know the vision of our organization? We should share something in the group, before sharing it with the organization (…).

When we reflect using the PAAR approach (Ghaye, 2008), we can better position ourselves as members of a team and of an organization, in a complex relational network; we can identify opportunities and constraints (and their origins), become aware of what supports us and hampers us in reaching our personal and professional goals, we can identify our expectations, reasoning at the same time according to a 'we' approach, open to represent ourselves as members of a team. Of course, the risk of translating the 'I and them' into a 'we and them' logic still remains, but it's a first fundamental step.

Further on, there is no possibility of responsible planning without critical awareness. Responsibility implies a certain degree of formalization, the acceptance of rules and rituals of negotiation. We can draw on our expectations to focus on our goals, but at the same time the challenge is to be able to embed our personal objectives in the framework of general aims in which we are working, acting in a responsible way. Moments in which people can share ideas and opinions with colleagues and then with the company's management might usefully be formalized thus:

> We thought to claim for free time in which we could organize our internal meetings, to share our proposals. It could be useful to recognize our value, and then build a 'collective vision' in order to select actual priorities. A formal moment, useful also to avoid subgroups dynamics (…) Claiming for a space in which we can talk to each other is also a matter of transparency.

Awareness led ECAP's coaches to better interpret the relationships between them and clients (e.g., self-empowering and maintaining the right emphatic distance). Mainly it influenced behaviors characterizing relational dynamics amongst colleagues (from competitive mistrust to appreciation of differences) and between colleagues and the organization to which they belonged (from 'claiming against the Empire' to active listening, to negotiating more flexible working conditions, to building sustainable participation). Future developments will depend on the evolution of agency/structure dynamics.

Characteristics of this development path clearly emerged by the words of protagonists participating in Lugano's follow-up project meeting:

> It all really begun at the right moment. The team just lived a wide series of changes, changes in professional roles, changes occurring in logistics, changes in working

> processes, we felt the need of a space for us, for reflecting on our practices.... I liked this proposal since the beginning, because I realized that we have been working on the basis of our needs and problems, such as normally occurs in reflective settings. As you know there's nothing more irritating for a trainer than feeling forced to listen top-down lessons, based on externally defined contents; we like to work according to our expectations and needs. Therefore [the laboratory] represented a suitable method, based on structured and consistent procedures, enabling participants to work on self defined contents.... But we are only at an initial stage. We exploited a range of tools, and we already benefit of positive achievements, in terms of perception of our roles, of group dynamics, of the way in which we relate with cultures and values of the organization...but they are as buds, a systematic implementation of the method seems to me far from being a reality, even because it implies an open discussion with the management. What has been brought in our daily work? For sure a better attitude towards valuation of positive things, with respect to constantly feel victims of problems, it's a fundamental change of perspective, but it's not yet consolidated.

Achievements are related to the possibility of working together, acting as a group: a heterogeneous team composed by individual profiles not an indistinct 'bunch of friends', but capable of building something together:

> Something is already there, doing it in a group, look to positive things, is easier if you work in a group; wake up every day trying to imagine a half-full glass depends from individual attitudes towards life, but making it in a group is a privileged moment. This experience gave us the possibility of meeting as a team of trainers; normally it's not happening, we act as individuals in an institution, we occasionally meet during pauses or during monthly meetings, but in that frame we discuss organizational aspects, we don't have any possibility of knowing one each other; it has been an unique opportunity of knowing my colleagues, from different points of view.... What's happening is that a collective reality grows up, and personally speaking I consider the team a resource...but in a team relational dynamics always play a role; you can have a coffee always with the same people, it's normal, you leave the other a part, and all these dynamics grow up; [the laboratory] helped us break this chain, gave us the possibility of looking one each other in a different way.

Achievements are at the same time related to appreciative logics and approaches, at least in two perspectives: considering triggers activating story telling (and proposals), and efforts made at dialogical level, expressing and debating opinions:

> Motivations behind proposals always refer to positive experiences...we moved from identification of positive conditions allowing a successful experience. Then it's clear that we begun to speak about positive things reaching at the end also problems and negative aspects... but the initial approach is what really counts.

This was in order to prepare constructive solutions. In the meantime, appreciative approach means also capability of taking in account interests, constraints and stakes affecting relational dynamics between colleagues and organization:

> In a top-down geared organization a project such as Reflect-OR is hard to imagine, it has no chance to be developed.... If your company allows you to develop this experience means that it is managed by open minded persons.

Participants in the laboratory recognized the need of overcoming 'I/we and them' philosophies, discussed during the second session:

> Why have certain proposals been successful? We activate a good strategy: demonstrating perseverance, monitoring delays, soliciting, but also recognizing prerogatives of the

> institutions, respecting hierarchies, involving people with enthusiasm, without overcoming, acting in a transparent way. We presented a proposal highlighting the added value both for the group and for the whole organization....

On the other side, responsible planning and critical awareness produced, at least initially, limited results, above all disappointing laboratory participants, because they perceived the gap between levels of reflection activated during the sessions and claims formalized to the management board. We can say that only heavy 'objects' passed through the funnel, during negotiations in the group. Many aspects proved to be difficult to translate in formal claims:

> All these themes, such as our interest in developing new projects, in managing new projects, or factors influencing internal communication and work division, some questions of organizational nature or other issues related to our professional identity in relationship with the organization... we try to put everything in the funnel, but only heavy objects passed through. This result seems to be perceived as disappointing. We worked on us, as a team, and it has been a success, but we left apart the organization.

Structure/agency dynamics clearly came to the fore. Feeling accepted as a team by the management and being aware of it represented a first step to activate a second level negotiation that was more mature and capable of modifying the structure, its written and non-written rules:

> Now that we have discussed, that we feel we share many ideas as a group, maybe we are ready to dialogue with 'the other' (the organization), that in effect is not properly other than us, because it simply includes us..... We face now the challenge of giving a name and consistency to lighter objects.

The challenge of valuing a new awareness of being a community of practitioners – part of the organization – in order to overcome superficial changes anchored to traditional levels of negotiations, began to become significant.

Rules and change management between unrest and participation

Looking at the socio-organizational dynamics in ECAP, through the lenses used for the COLs' case (see Tomassini and alias, already quoted) allows some further considerations about the results of Reflect-OR experience in Switzerland.

A first set of considerations can be briefly provided in relation to the characteristics of the *structure/agency* dyad in the Swiss case, putting the focus on the interrelations between its regulatory environment and mission statements, on one side, and the 'agentic' aspects implied in guidance work and organizations. As already underlined in previous sections of this paper, the Swiss system at the national level, both considering lifelong career guidance and public-private partnership in employment services (as in our case), is characterized by high functional stability, wide social recognition and acceptance, internal mechanisms of change related to both the social demand of guidance services and the evolution of conceptual backgrounds and techniques in this field. The overall Swiss system is in fact an interesting hybrid between the highly privatized Anglo-Saxon model and the more public-orientated German system. Public institutions and agencies at the cantonal level coexist with – and provide regulations and financing to – private institutions. At the local level, ECAP is a key player among the latter: its mission is to carry out specific training and guidance activities

Figure 3. Tags (key words) cloud: synthesizing appreciative inquiry.

for well-identified target groups, in particular for people who recently lost their job and are forced to quickly re-employ themselves before the welfare grants' expiration. In practice, ECAP has to take in charge unemployed persons, sent by the local labor authority, and to accompany them in processes in which training and guidance on one side and active job search on the other side are mutually reinforcing.

Such a mission is structurally different from the one of the Roman COLs, the other field of Reflect-OR's implementation to which we referred earlier. COLs' mission is in fact related to wide population segments (including short- and long-term unemployed and 'weak' social groups such as women in midlife, socially disadvantaged people, migrants, etc.). COLs' clients autonomously address the guidance services while the latter assume them as subjects of direct relations aimed at providing information and (in some cases) guidance counseling, without any specific mandate regarding the final results of such activities.

In comparison with the Roman colleagues, the ECAP guidance practitioners operate in a much more structured and homogeneous context. We already stressed the importance of acting under mandate of a local authority holding different levels of control on goals and even, to a certain extent, on means used to reach such goals. Moreover, ECAP has a consolidated tradition in terms of history, culture and accumulated know-how and routines. It represents the modern evolution of a former trade-union-owned assistance institution for Italian migrants in Switzerland. Its present activities, mainly oriented towards adults' training and guidance, follow (and in some cases are still linked to) previous vocational training initiatives, addressed to group of workers or would-be workers in different sectors. ECAP as an organizational system is connoted by structuring properties which entail: a significant stability of practical knowledge in use ('how things are to be done'); clearly established work routines, inscribed in actors' memory and behavior; continuity of the social practices linked to the institutional aims; continuous informal adjustment of the capabilities needed for performing such practices, and even for innovating them over time according to changes occurring on the side of clients and of mandatory authority as well.

The pace of such changes has been significantly accelerated in the past few years. At present, different stress factors condition the ECAP workers' 'agency', and trigger it at the same time, pushing towards faster transformations as far as knowledge in-use, routines, performances, capabilities and attitudes towards innovation are concerned. Starting from very different background conditions in comparison with those observable in the Roman case, ECAP 'coaches' – feeling a bit like adult trainers, a bit like guidance practitioners – find themselves in the midst of a complex transition phase, requiring clearer awareness about the depth of the occurring changes. Several aspects of such an awareness have emerged in the reflective workshops during the implementation of the Reflect-OR project. They can be re-read through the scheme already used for the analysis of the *empowerment processes*.

Concerning professional identity construction, ECAP coaches have reflected several times on the changes taking place at this level. The now prevailing role behavior appears less and less linked to given sets of attitudes and capabilities and largely connoted in terms of multiplicity and continuous innovation:

> The mask we wear is different in relations to the situations: in the past, as we lived in a stable group we used to take for granted that people [the clients, the mandatory authority] see us only in a given way. Now we realize that it's important to be able to offer different images of ourselves.

The activity routines are also changing over time, especially because of variances in clients' needs:

> There are different repetitive aspects in this work, but it also allows me – and requires from me – to continuously 'refresh' my specificities.

The opportunities for competence development are wider than in the past and largely linked to experiential factors and work-based learning:

> Despite our basic theory and formal training we always have to privilege intuition and capture the moment. This is the way our competence really grew up.

The relations with clients represent a fundamental benchmark regarding competence development and a source of relevant questions at this regard:

> How can I be able to motivate and to instill the importance of self-motivation? Did I say the right things in order to help the person in front of me in keeping alive his/her own self-motivation? Am I on the right track at this regard?

Moreover, the chances for professional growth are seen as resulting from both individual and collective efforts. A potential community of practice has emerged over time and it is now challenged by the arrival of several newcomers. Many consolidated intra-group relations are pushed towards uncertain changes; however, the sense of the community resists and is perceived as valuable per se, from both the internal and the external viewpoint:

> Of course everybody likes to go and have a coffee with somebody that is nice. This way some levels of complicity emerge.... This is not wrong, but we should do more.... We

should be more visible as group and then we should try to be acknowledged outside. This is a relevant improvement objective. We have to make efforts about it.

The emotional life at work and the need to foster higher levels of emotional intelligence are clearly perceived within the group, especially regarding the relations with clients, very often source of anxiety and risks:

> Clients learn ways of knowing and trusting us. Sometimes they try to take the lead in the relationship and to instrumentally use personal issues, anxieties and fears. Sometimes they make us feel unable to handle the situations. One has to know how to put boundaries. We must be guides ...and we must be able to manage ourselves and to help them [the clients] in putting themselves into play.

The transformational effects of reflection have been realized at the end of the workshops. It has been very much appreciated that the Reflect-OR project attempted, in many ways successfully, to systematize reflection and to put it in the service of better work conditions and prospects:

> Because of the project we had chances for appreciating what we are able do and, for the first time, for establishing an explicit common reflection about the relevant changes that recently took place in our work environment. Exchange, support and sharing are surely useful for everybody. Now we are motivated in putting us into play and to improve our openness to better relations with colleagues.

PAAR in practice: lessons to learn

Achievements of the laboratory, potentialities as well as limits of reflective practices coping with change in organizational patterns and professional identity, must be finally read under the lens of the spaces and contradictions which actually emerged, as well as of requirements needed to enable experiential learning through participative appreciative action and reflection methods.

First of all we should bear in mind that we are in the middle of an uncertain evolution in the dynamics affecting structure/agency relationship in the framework of the ECAP training center. PAAR opened windows and reflective frames and let laboratory participants experience new ways of developing reflection, gaining awareness of their identity and role. They learned to appreciate positive outcomes of their job, rooting in positive stories, claims and proposals addressed to the organization. Management discovered new ways for setting and solving organizational challenges, potentially effective, but implying a certain degree of transformation in leadership styles and patterns. Globally considered, actors seem now looking for consolidating new relational frames. Contradictions are still there, both considering operators' temptation of excluding the management from reflective discussions, channeling proposals in a narrow negotiation of daily job arrangements, that could paradoxically meet management need of restoring an affordable hierarchical control, reducing at the same time autonomous learning spaces opened by the laboratory.

The Swiss case study is the opposite of Rome's situation. It allowed us to identify braking factors and constraints hampering 'change' that emerge in a structured and well-established organizational environment. Shifts in professional identities, induced under the pressure of external pushes, could be a trigger for change. We found that our reflections helped to enhance our self esteem, thus diminishing defensive attitudes. Hierarchical and rigid structure of mandates, limiting autonomy and participative decision-making processes, as well as bureaucratic monitoring and evaluation systems, based on summative criteria and indicators, produced a 'sense of injustice' and influenced in a negative way, the perception operators have of career development logics. Critical attitudes and self reflection are likely to be refused, perceived as evidences of weakness and unsecure behavior. From one side, clients' satisfaction, and from the other side acceptance of institutional regulations, became the reference point orienting *structure/agency* dynamics. The organization pays obviously attention to the latter, while operators look at clients' reactions, trying to 'capture' positive feedback in order to reinforce their self-confidence and find 'recognition'. Doing so they risk reducing the right 'empathic distance that should characterize their guidance and counseling action. On the other hand the need for 'surviving' in a structured organization and in a working team determines the emergence of compromises and relational artifacts. Sometimes we had the impression that tensions, conflicts and competitive behaviors remained hidden under the surface of formal participative appreciation 'rhetoric'.

Beyond the peculiarities of the context, clearly underlined in this paper, ECAP's laboratory helped us understand the relevance of some general requirements for a successful exploitation of reflective practices, both at individual and organizational level. At the individual level we needed open-minded people whose personal self esteem has been nurtured and enabled by critical 'reflective attitudes', counter balancing natural tendencies (above all in group settings) to activating self-defense rituals and behaviors. The capability of critical thinking and ability to sustain others' regard fosters membership to a community of practitioners, feeds a solid professional identity. Satisfactory incentives (enhancing affective dimensions of learning) also play a relevant role, as well as individual attitude and readiness to cope with cognitive challenges (changing and unstable roles should be conceived as learning triggers not only threats).

On the other hand, organizational requirements come to the fore. Independence and 'strength' of the organization, towards 'market' logics (in a very delicate sector, as in public-private guidance services) plays a fundamental role. Courage, sufficient autonomy of the organization in defining procedures and plans to organize the team and deliver services, are to be valued, avoiding in any case 'self defense' attitudes of the management, always present also in relationships between organizations and its members. Visibility of the mission, based on a constant 'narration' of history and achievements, reinforces a sense of belonging and enables mutual understanding, facilitating constructive dynamics. A 'delegating' leadership style, fostering shared responsibilities and participation, seems to be more adequate than a structured functional hierarchy, to promote peer-reviewing practices. However, leaders should not skip to manage in a transparent way all rituals and dynamics normally affecting any working group. The demand for transparency and recognition by management and by the organization emerged stronger at the end of the laboratory. This implies that in order to develop all potentialities of PAAR, effective organizational strategies should assure a clear career and professionalization management system, based on shared criteria, indicators and open confrontation practices.

Acknowledgements

In writing the article, authors valued the great amount of materials and protocols, collected and systematized by Elisa Cavicchiolo and Simona Marchi, and also inputs produced by a group of Ticino's Reflect-OR laboratory participants, that met several times without RLIs and

ECAP facilitators during 12 months of work. In addition a precious contribution has been given by witnesses participating to Lugano's follow-up conference, held in September 2010, particularly by Barbara Favoni and Ingo Tamagni, acting as spokespersons of the whole group of participants.

Notes

1. See in this special issue Massimo Tomassini, Antonella Barile, Eleonora Fiumara and Paola Scarpello, *Empowering people through reframing: experiences of guidance practitioners in a public network of career centres.*
2. Massimo Tomassini, Antonella Barile, Eleonora Fiumar and Paola Scarpello, *Empowering people through reframing: experiences of guidance practitioners in a public network of career centres*

References

Ghaye, T. (2008). *An introduction to participatory and appreciative action research (PAAR): Some principles and processes.* Gloucester: New Vista Publications.

Giddens, A. (1979). *Central problems in social theory. Action, structure and contradiction in social analysis.* Berkley: UCLA Press.

Illeris, K. (2007). *Laering.* [How we learn. Learning and non learning in school and beyond] Roskilde: Roskilde University Press.

Lave, J., & Wenger, E. (1991). *Situated learning: Legitimate peripheral participation.* New York: Cambridge University Press.

Mezirow, J. (2000). Learning to think like an adult: Core conceptions of transformation theory. In J. Mezirow and associates (Eds.) *Learning as transformation: Critical perspectives on a theory in progress* San Francisco: Jossey Bass.

Soini, H. (2000, October). *Critical learning incident technique as a research method for studying student learning,* Paper presented at the Workshop Qualitative Research in Psychology, Blauberen (Germany).

Stroobants, H., Chambers, P., & Clarke, B. (2007). *Reflective journeys. A fieldbook for facilitating life-long learning in vocational education and training.* Rome: Istituto Tagliacarne.

Index

Page numbers in **bold** type refer to figures
Page numbers in *italic* type refer to tables
Page numbers followed by 'n' refer to notes